THE PERFECT CORPORATE BOARD

A HANDBOOK FOR MASTERING THE UNIQUE CHALLENGES OF SMALL-CAP COMPANIES

ADAM J. EPSTEIN

New York   Chicago   San Francisco   Lisbon   London
Madrid   Mexico City   New Delhi   San Juan
Seoul   Singapore   Sydney   Toronto

1 2 3 4 5 6 7 8 9 10   DOC/DOC   1 8 7 6 5 4 3 2

ISBN   978-0-07-179954-6
MHID   0-07-179954-0

e-ISBN   978-0-07-179955-3
e-MHID   0-07-179955-9

This publication is designed to provide accurate and authoritative information in regard to the subject matter covered. It is sold with the understanding that neither the author nor the publisher is engaged in rendering legal, accounting, securities trading, or other professional services. If legal advice or other expert assistance is required, the services of a competent professional person should be sought.
> —From a Declaration of Principles Jointly Adopted by a Committee of the American Bar Association and a Committee of Publishers and Associations

Library of Congress Cataloging-in-Publication Data

Epstein, Adam.
    The perfect corporate board : a handbook for mastering the unique challenges of small-cap companies / by Adam Epstein.
        p. cm.
    ISBN-13: 978-0-07-179954-6 (alk. paper)
    ISBN-10: 0-07-179954-0 (alk. paper)
    1. Small business—Finance.   2. Small business—Management.   3. Boards of directors. 4. Small capitalization stocks. I. Title.
    HG4027.7.E587 2013
    658.4'22—dc23   2012034111

CONTENTS

ACKNOWLEDGMENTS

This book would not have been possible without the contributions and support of many people.

First and foremost, I'm indebted to Alexandra Lajoux and Jennifer Ashkenazy for believing in the value of the project and for the energy, direction, and expertise necessary for it to become a reality.

For their generous contributions of time, expertise, and data, I'm indebted to Tim Bacci, David Collins, Steven Dresner, David Enzer, John Heilshorn, Tim Keating, David Lee, Mitch Levine, Dan Lonkevich, Jon Merriman, Larry Stambaugh, and Adam Steinhauer.

For their thoughtful support, I'm indebted to Eric Bark, Paul Barrett, Kevin Epstein, Pamela Friedman, James Gellert, Brian Greenstein, Dian Griesel, Karol Hochman, Lance Ignon, Neal Kaufman, Janet Kerr, Judson Kleinman, Max and Lila Kleinman, Neil Koehler, Adam Lyon, Scott and Veronique Markewitz, John Pimentel, Jonathan Read, Alan Sheinwald, Joseph Smith, Linda Sweeney, David and Reily Urban, and Judy Warner.

For being the best role models anyone could ever have, I'm indebted to Ira and Miriam Epstein, Reuben Epstein, and Wolfgang Lert.

And, to my wife and best friend Connie, nothing is possible without you.

FOREWORD

Alexandra R. Lajoux

"Lost on the Moon," the classic group exercise, begins with a bang—the imaginary crash of a spaceship. The goal for participants is to get back to the mother ship on a transporter ASAP. Astronauts in the scenario have 15 items, but because of space constraints, they can't take them all. What should they pack? Choices include a box of matches, oxygen tanks, water, a compass, and so forth. NASA asks participants to rank their choices from 1 (most important) to 15 (least important); responses are then checked against NASA's answer sheet. As it turns out, a compass and matches rank only a 14 and 15 for NASA; they are useless in outer space. By contrast, oxygen tanks and water rank a high 1 and a 2, respectively. Without them one would perish.

This vivid scene is not unlike the critical situation facing small-cap boards today. They are small groups of five to seven men and women working together to survive and thrive in new territories under virtually "life-threatening" conditions season after season. As Adam Epstein says so eloquently in the introduction to this much-needed guidebook, "Small-cap directors frequently operate in environments in which alternatives and flexibility are replaced by a cognizance that even seemingly innocuous decision making can have business-ending consequences." How true this is. In a typical year, more than 100 public companies will file for bankruptcy. That's nearly one in ten of all business bankruptcies—a high level considering that public companies comprise only a tiny percentage of the broader business scene. What makes public companies, particularly smaller ones, vulnerable to failure?

It's a matter of stakes. They are higher the smaller a company is, Epstein notes. If small-cap directors set the wrong priorities—go for the matches and the compass instead of the oxygen and water, so to speak—they may face business failure. Behind this analogy is a significant scientific point. "Lost on the Moon" and similar survival-exercise research show the importance of group wisdom in avoiding failure. This is because, "The group's effort is almost always an improvement over its average individual resource, and often it is better than even the best individual contribution," wrote Jay Hall in *Psychology Today* more than 40 years ago. Based on this finding, a company can benefit simply by using its board as a group to solve problems.

But here is the challenge. In some situations, it is not always easy to identify the problem (as in, "We have crashed,") or the solution (as in, "We need to get back to the mother ship with good supplies.") Also, on some boards, the collective group wisdom cannot find the solution as a group because one individual is doing all the talking.

That is why Adam Epstein's book is so valuable. It identifies the key challenges to small-cap growth and offers solutions to resolve them. In doing so, it empowers all small-cap directors to play a vital role in moving their companies beyond the next horizon—with the right supplies.

INTRODUCTION

Over the last 5 years, companies like Lehman Brothers, Country-wide, AIG, Goldman Sachs, Microsoft, Apple, News Corp., Yahoo!, and Hewlett-Packard have collectively made as many headlines associated with corporate governance as they have for their underlying businesses. Every step and misstep of these boards are dissected and debated by investors large and small, media, regulators, directors, and academics. Much has been said and written on the subject, and the attention will continue unabated inasmuch as the stakes are high. Interestingly, though, virtually nothing is said or written about corporate governance in a very different subset of companies— one where the stakes are even higher.

With all the emphasis upon well-known large-cap multinationals, it's easy for even a well-informed person to overlook that in excess of 7 out of every 10 U.S.-listed public companies have market capitalizations that are less than $500 million. More specifically, and in stark contrast to the S&P 500 which benchmarks nearly $6 trillion, the median equity value of a U.S.-listed public company is only $450 million. Consequently, not only is the majority of public companies small, but the vast majority of directors govern small public companies.

Why should anyone care about these small public companies? The most important reason is **jobs**. For example, a July 2010 Kauffman Foundation report on job creation concluded that without fast-growing, early-stage companies, domestic job growth over the last 35 years would actually be negative. And with 92 percent of job creation in early-stage companies occurring subsequent to their initial public offerings (IPOs), according to National Venture Capital Association statistics, the health and well-being of small public companies will always play a material role in the U.S. economy.

To date, however, the national corporate governance dialogue has been fixated on issues faced by large public companies because there are fewer of them, they are the most well-known, and they have the most resources. The by-product, however, of this myopia is that discussion of governance best practices has been "one size fits all," notwithstanding the fact that small public companies are routinely stymied by unique governance issues for which there is no objective, practical guidance. Just as operating a $450 million company is conspicuously dissimilar to operating a $450 billion company, governing the former is a different undertaking from governing the latter—a lot different.

ENTERPRISE RISK IS RELATIVE

Small-cap[1] companies are, in a sense, immune-suppressed versions of their larger counterparts; that is, a failed clinical trial, an adverse jury verdict, or a product recall might be little more than routine impediments to a company on the Dow, but to a $150 million company with a tenuous balance sheet and stock that isn't sufficiently liquid to facilitate a lifeline of further growth capital, any of those challenges could prove insurmountable. Just as healthy balance sheets and robust cash flow at larger public companies provide, among other things, strategic alternatives and financial flexibility, the opposite is also true. Small-cap directors frequently operate in environments in which alternatives and flexibility are replaced by a cognizance that even seemingly innocuous decision making can have business-ending consequences.

Additionally, small-cap directors are often required to analyze myriad issues that would never even see the light of day in a Fortune 500 boardroom. You would have to attend only a few small-cap board meetings to realize that, contrary to the "axioms" often taught in graduate schools and governance seminars, the bright line which separates governance issues from management issues isn't actually a bright line at all. That is, risks and consequences are relative; an issue requiring no board oversight at one company could well require extensive board action at another.

Imagine, for example, that you are one of seven directors on the board of ABCD, a $250 million Nasdaq-listed technology company that has been sued by a Fortune 500 company for patent infringement. Although the intellectual property at issue isn't central to ABCD's present or future business, the time and cost of a protracted litigation could have austere consequences for ABCD. Moreover, and as is quite common in small-cap companies, ABCD doesn't have any in-house counsel or legal department, and its officers lack litigation experience. For most large public companies, the basic elements of defending noncore patent litigation (i.e., hiring counsel, negotiating fees, developing litigation strategy, etc.) would hardly garner active board oversight for two reasons: (1) most large public companies have extensive in-house legal departments with the requisite resources and expertise; and (2) there is minimal, if any, enterprise risk posed by this type of litigation. ABCD's directors, however, govern in a dramatically different setting, where management's lack of litigation expertise and the potentially ruinous enterprise risks compel active oversight.

RESOURCES OR LACK THEREOF

To add to the challenge that many small-cap directors face governing in heightened enterprise risk ecosystems, the resources available are often a fraction of what large public company boards have at their disposal. Consider that:(1) the total compensation for a single director at a Fortune 100 company might eclipse the total compensation for an entire small-cap board; (2) many small-cap companies have half as many directors as large public companies do; and (3) unlike the annual seven-digit expenditures often paid to consultants and board advisors at large public companies, many small-cap boards have no such resources.

As a result of these resource constraints, the composition of small-cap boards is also often quite different from those at large public companies. Large public company boards often have more than a dozen directors and include former politicians, industry regulators, military leaders, and capital markets, corporate finance, legal, and governance experts. Conversely, small-cap boards are often less than half the size and are principally composed of directors possessing mission critical expertise; that is, directors who can help with what matters most to nascent businesses—revenue generation, supply chain optimization, clinical trial design, and so on. To be sure, many small-cap boards would benefit dramatically from political, regulatory, capital markets, corporate finance, legal, and governance acumen. But large boards aren't practical for small, nimble companies, and they are far too costly. Accordingly, small-cap directors must often simply do more with considerably less.

VARIABLE EXPERIENCE

In addition to ubiquitous enterprise risk and constrained resources, small-cap directors often govern companies in which management teams have considerably less experience operating public companies than what you'd characteristically find in larger public companies; that is, intelligence, sophistication, talent, and success notwithstanding, there are literally thousands of either first-time or comparatively inexperienced public company CEOs and CFOs operating small-cap companies.

Moreover, the quality and expertise of professional service providers focused on small-cap companies are highly variable. And while large public companies tend to select from a comparatively limited pool of blue-chip banking, auditing, and law firms, there are hundreds of small-cap professional service providers.

Accordingly, just as ABCD's directors were compelled to actively participate in rudimentary elements of its patent litigation, the majority of small-cap directors must eschew the level of deference routinely afforded highly experienced management teams and service providers at larger public companies in favor of a considerably more hands-on approach.

THREE-DIMENSIONAL CHESS

As if heightened enterprise risk, lean staffing, resource constraints, and hands-on governing weren't enough, small-cap directors are routinely faced with another impediment that is the proverbial elephant in the room—growth capital. Simply put, the primary distinguishing factor between the majority of small-cap companies on the one hand and mid- and large-cap companies on the other is cash flow. Or in the case of most small-cap companies—negative cash flow. Since most small-cap companies don't generate sufficient cash flow to finance their operations and growth, vast amounts of time and resources are focused on corporate finance.

But unlike larger corporations which raise capital electively and from positions of strength, most small-cap companies enjoy no such luxuries. Rather, for most small-cap companies infusions of outside capital are mandatory, and there is often little latitude with respect to timing. Accordingly, small-cap directors are regularly beset by a treadmill of sorts that always seems to move a little faster and a little more uphill—raising sufficient growth capital on the least dilutive terms to fund current operations, and then taking the necessary steps to position the company for future such financings. And, in many cases, they do that again and again. As evidenced by the fact that the median market capitalization of U.S.-listed public companies is only $450 million, the number of companies successfully navigating that treadmill is dwarfed by those that are either mired in stasis or soon to be ejected off the back of the treadmill.

To be sure, part of the reason why the median market capitalization of U.S.-listed public companies is only $450 million is that there are scores of small-cap companies that simply shouldn't be public companies at all (i.e., they are too nascent, or their growth profiles no longer justify the expense of being public)—a topic that could easily fill another book. Moreover, there are also myriad small-cap companies that habitually overpromise and underdeliver and thus suffer from minimal investor interest. But when you subtract the small-cap companies that shouldn't be public and/or are otherwise operationally snookered, what's left is a meaningful subset of companies that should be able to grow far in excess of a $450 million valuation—but don't. Why?

There isn't an easy answer. If you ask those who interface regularly with small-cap officers and directors (i.e., investment bankers, lawyers, auditors, investor relations professionals, equity analysts, and institutional investors), they will tell you that one of the least appreciated reasons why otherwise promising small-cap companies fail to graduate to mid-cap size and beyond is the systemic failure of directors to adequately appreciate and understand the nuances of corporate finance and capital markets. Jack Nicklaus, a famous golfer, once stated that you can't win a tournament by shooting a low number in the first of four rounds, but you can certainly lose the tournament with a terrible first round. Similarly, promising small-cap companies can't guarantee success with smart financing, but they can certainly forestall or destroy an otherwise successful trajectory with terrible financing or a poorly conceived capital markets strategy.

More specifically, the unique governance issues that result from serial capital raising in the small-cap ecosystem are a complex, three-dimensional chessboard, where each of the subject matters—corporate finance, capital markets, and professional service providers—are interrelated. To get a sense of these intertwined dynamics, consider the following illustration.

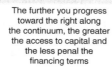

Illiquid stock no research coverage, deficient balance sheet, unknown service providers

Liquid stock, extensive research coverage, healthy balance sheet, well-known service providers

The further you progress toward the right along the continuum, the greater the access to capital and the less penal the financing terms

For better or worse, the majority of small-cap companies fall further toward the left side of the continuum than the right, thus making access to growth capital more challenging and financing terms more penal—neither of which is good for shareholders when growth capital infusions are often a continuing necessity. This, in turn, places a premium on boards that not only acknowledge the austerity of this sliding scale but, perhaps more importantly, can navigate the three dimensions with aplomb. But while the need for this multifaceted sophistication in small-cap boardrooms is high, it is the absence of this sophistication that market observers underscore.

There are four reasons why this dynamic exists and continues:

1. *Resources.* As discussed earlier, many small-cap companies have limited governance resources, which translates into smaller boards. When you consider that most small-cap boards have between five to seven directors and you subtract the chief executive officer and the audit chairperson, you are often left with between three and five incremental independent directors. Since revenue growth, product innovation, strategic alliances, clinical trials, supply chain, and so on are all mission critical for small public companies, there is an understandably strong bias in favor of adding directors with those kinds of backgrounds. Correspondingly, there is little latitude, either financially

or structurally, to add corporate finance or capital markets specialists to small-cap boards.

2. *Limited pool.* In addition to financial and structural constraints, there is a limited pool of prospective directors who understand the intricacies of small-cap finance and capital markets and who are also qualified for and interested in board service.

3. *Myopia.* Historically, corporate governance thought leaders have all shared large-cap backgrounds and foci. Accordingly, the vast majority of books, magazines, online content, webinars, and continuing education seminars are focused on corporate governance issues faced by large public companies. The result is that many small-cap directors have few resources, if any, that address their unique governance challenges.

4. *Disincentives.* There is a multi-billion dollar small-cap corporate finance industry comprised of investment banks, institutional investors, attorneys, and so on, that profits from the status quo.

LEVELING THE PLAYING FIELD

Lest anyone draw inferences to the contrary, the vast majority of small-cap directors are not only intelligent, successful, and dedicated, but they also spend considerable amounts of time for not a lot of money trying to do their bests to advance shareholder value. However, it's hard to make up for experience you don't have. Accordingly, and understandably, faced with making highly specialized capital markets and corporate finance decisions, many small-cap directors typically take one of three routes: (1) they outsource the decision making to service providers; (2) they defer to the board member who has the most relevant experience; or (3) they simply do their best to make sound decisions based on the facts and circumstances at hand.

The first of the three routes is the most common, but it can also be the least effective. In the best-case scenario, seminal governance decisions are effectively being made by attorneys or investor relations professionals who mightn't be particularly better suited to make them than the directors. In the worst-case scenario, decisions are being made by investment bankers who often have a material conflict of interest (i.e., they get paid only if the board agrees to do what the bankers are proposing). And the success of the second and third routes is dependent upon directors simply doing their best with the experience they have—or don't have. Succinctly, it's not a level playing field for most small-cap boards.

The goal of this book is to fill a conspicuous void—to provide for the first time a practical tool for small-cap directors (especially those who govern companies with $500 million market capitalizations and under—the majority of public companies) to use in order to more effectively analyze their unique governance challenges. To level the playing field, if you will. The book is designed to be used as a continuing resource; a handbook of common albeit uniquely small-cap situations with a corresponding summary of suggested analyses intended for quick reference and more in-depth discussions of the reasoning behind the analyses intended to stimulate board dialogue.

Of equal importance is what this book is not. There are countless exhaustively researched articles and treatises on corporate governance best practices; this book will contribute little to those. Though audit, nominating, and compensation committee best practices are critical for directors of all sizes of public companies to master, those resources are ubiquitous and readily available to all directors. On the other hand, the content of this book presupposes adherence to existing governance best practices and (figuratively speaking) incorporates them all by reference. Simply put, it wouldn't help small-cap directors at all to have yet another book that repurposes oft-repeated governance axioms because those axioms don't address many of the day-to-day obstacles small-cap directors actually face.

Ultimately, being a small-cap director is an exercise in entrepre-neurial governance—being nimble, doing more with less, and shep-herding an asset against long odds for risk-embracing shareholders. The odds, however, are needlessly long in part because small-cap directors lack the targeted, practical guidance they require. At a time when U.S. public companies need to provide more jobs to Americans and compete more efficiently on the international stage, *The Perfect Corporate Board: A Handbook for Mastering the Unique Challenges of Small-Cap Companies* is an effort to maximize decision making that assists in both areas.

PART 1

CORPORATE FINANCE

There are few corporate actions that small-cap officers and directors approach with more trepidation than financings. And for good reason. Financings are expensive, dilutive, time-consuming, and often stressful. For the vast majority of small-cap companies,[1] they are a routine necessity.

For better or worse, no two financings are ever the same. At the macro level, political and economic forces both in the United States and abroad conspire to create capital markets volatility; sometimes the volatility helps financings, and sometimes it hurts. At the micro level, industries thrive and suffer cyclically, and thus fall in and out of favor in the capital markets. At the company level, officers and directors come and go, financial statements strengthen and weaken, and stock prices rise and fall with varying degrees of liquidity. At a more granular level still, officers and directors are not always in agreement, and to further complicate matters professional service providers aren't either.

Ironically, one of the few constants in this milieu is that small-cap officers and directors can more often than not be their own worst enemies when it comes to corporate finance; that is, they often unwittingly conspire to make financings more expensive, more dilutive, more time-consuming, and more stressful than need be, best intentions notwithstanding. While there are a few companies that are either so easy or virtually impossible to finance that a board's collective corporate finance IQ isn't terribly impactful one way or another, the vast majority of small-cap financings fall in between the two extremes, and are exacting exercises for small-cap boards. Indeed, most small-cap financings arise out of conspicuously mixed bags of facts and circumstances in companies that have very little margin for error. You might say that many are exercises in making lemonade out of lemons.

To illustrate the point statistically, consider Figure 1.1 depicting all the capital raised in the small-cap ecosystem in 2011. What's particularly instructive to note is the direct correlation between the size of the company and the number of financings. More specifically, approximately 82 percent of the financings were undertaken by companies with less than $250 million in market capitalizations, and approximately 66 percent of the financings were undertaken by companies with less than $100 million in market capitalizations. These aren't statistical aberrations; in 2010, according to PrivateRaise, approximately 87 percent of small-cap financings were undertaken by companies with less than $250 million in market capitalizations, and the figure was 83 percent for 2009. In other words, the companies that are the most challenging to finance are doing the most financings.

Figure 1.1 **Small-Cap Financings, 2011**

Market cap size	Number of financings	Aggregate dollar value
$50 million and under	487	$4,368,992,441
$50 million to $99 million	191	$3,285,132,154
$100 million to $249 million	174	$4,119,100,255
$250 million to $499 million	68	$2,084,206,740
$500 million to $999 million	57	$4,616,084,027
$1 billion to $4.9 billion	56	$7,018,592,253
Total	1,033	$25,492,107,870

Source: PrivateRaise, a service of DealFlow Media.

Given the multidimensional complexities of small-cap corporate finance, it would stand to reason that the path to a better understanding for directors is beset by convolution. But just as finding your way through a new city is often made considerably easier by learning a handful of main thoroughfares, the ability of small-cap directors to excel at analyzing corporate finance issues starts with a single proposition—being realistic. *Brutally* realistic, at that.

Anyone who has spent considerable time as a banker, lawyer, auditor, investor relations professional, or institutional investor in the small-cap realm has a favorite "cautionary tale" about a company that displayed such poor judgment in pursuit of financing that it either flirted with insolvency (sometimes more than once) or actually went bankrupt (sometimes more than once). It can be hard to determine what's more alarming about these stories—the sheer number of them, or the board actions or omissions that precipitated the failure. Year after year these corporate finance "lowlights" give way to a discernible pattern. While nothing replaces the need for a thorough understanding of corporate finance and capital markets, many small-cap directors often get off on the proverbial wrong foot simply by failing to be realistic about what matters most about their circumstances.

Consequently, and prior to delving into the more granular issues associated with each chronological step of a financing, it's critical to create a realistic foundation before approaching a financing in the boardroom. More specifically, each of the 10 axioms below are continually disregarded by many small-cap officers and directors to such an extent that they regrettably form the starting point for hundreds of cautionary tales:

1. *Be realistic about economic, political, judicial, and legislative environments.* Every company, size notwithstanding, is impacted by macro elements like these that are out of any director's control. The **key point** here is not to dwell on such issues, but to be cognizant of them and to actively discuss them during board meetings. While macro issues affect all companies, the smaller the company, the more impactful the issues, especially if the timing of a seminal ruling or announcement happens to correspond with a time when financing is required. Simply put, small-cap directors in particular have an obligation to keep abreast of macro factors that can impact the businesses they govern and their ability to garner financing. For example, if a biofuels company waits to raise further growth capital until a few months before Congress intends to vote on the extension of various green subsidies, the directors shouldn't be surprised that the financing terms they are offered are so penal.

2. *Be realistic about overall stock market strength or weakness.* Whether directors have capital markets backgrounds or not, they need to be aware of whether the stock market is reaching new highs, trading sideways, or plumbing new lows. There is nothing here that can't be found by occasionally reading

the *The Wall Street Journal*. Boards regularly assume to the detriment of shareholders that good times, for example, will continue to roll and consequently delay financings until an even higher stock price is achieved, or they delay corporate housekeeping matters like obtaining shareholder approval for expanding authorized share counts. The stock market will go up and down, but the only certainty for many small-cap companies is that they will require further capital. Therefore, there are two **key points** here: (a) consider strengthening the company's balance sheet when the market is strong whether you need the extra capital currently or not; and (b) if you must raise money in a weak market, be realistic about your circumstances, take your "medicine," and live for another day.

3. *Be realistic about whether an industry is in or out of favor.*
   Like lapel sizes, industries move in and out of favor.
   Directors need to stay apprised of what's happening in
   their industries because small-cap companies must take
   advantage of cyclicality to raise money. The **key point** here is
   that sometimes it's best for the shareholders for a company
   to raise capital when the industry is in favor, even if this
   situation doesn't correspond with capital needs or company
   performance. In other words, a rising tide lifts all boats.
   Conversely, the board should consider augmenting the
   amount of capital raised, if possible, when it's low tide.

4. *Be realistic about how your competitors and peers are financing
   themselves.* More often than not in small-cap finance, companies
   garner similar amounts of capital and similar financing terms to
   similarly situated companies (i.e., industry, market capitalization,
   exchange, trading volume) that recently raised capital. The **key
   point** here is that small-cap officers and directors need to be
   better students of financings that have recently been undertaken

by similarly situated companies. There are no excuses for failing to do so, and it can't be overstated how much time, energy, and money can be saved by not falling prey to misguided expectations developed in the absence of the facts garnered from this.

5. *Be realistic about the strength of the management team.* The strength and experience of small-cap management teams are highly variable, and nothing puts these abilities on display quite the way a financing does. Directors, for many reasons, need to be especially realistic about not only the strengths and weaknesses of officers, but also about how they are perceived by investors. The **key points** here are: (a) directors need to make time to watch management present the company to investors, or request that management present the company to the board; (b) directors need to be mindful of whether management has any discernible experience raising capital for small public companies, because many small-cap management teams do not; and (c) the board should consider asking investment banks to provide feedback about management performance in connection with financings directly to the independent board members.

6. *Be realistic about financial strength and performance.* Many small-cap directors fail in this regard because they lack sufficient ability to view companies through the eyes of investors. While directors of all sizes of companies can benefit dramatically from better understanding how retail and institutional investors think, it's especially important in the small-cap ecosystem because, for example, balance sheets are often encumbered with complex derivative instruments like warrants, or highly structured notes which can dramatically impact investor interest or prospective financing terms. Moreover, while a board might be of the opinion that 100 percent sequential growth justifies a

higher valuation, investors might still simply see a small, very risky company. The **key point** here is that the more directors understand how investors will perceive a company's strength and performance, the less time, money, and energy will be wasted on and around a financing.

7. *Be realistic about the company's capital markets profile.* One of the anomalies of the small-cap ecosystem that's least understood by officers and directors (but near and dear to the hearts of investment bankers and institutional investors) is that, unlike in the mid- and large-cap realms, there are good companies that have terrible stocks, and terrible companies that have good stocks. This happens because some companies that are executing well end up being lightly traded, underfollowed by equity analysts, and mostly unknown to the institutional community. Conversely, there are companies with far less impressive execution that trade a dramatic amount of volume every day, have comparatively high valuations, and are well known to the investment community. To state the obvious, it's best to be a good company and have a good stock. The **key points** here are that: (a) directors need to better understand, for a variety reasons, which bucket their company fits in; and (b) directors need to better understand what their company's stock price, trading volume, and market capitalization mean to investors and how they impact the type of financing that can be transacted.

8. *Be realistic about the company's use of prior financing proceeds.* Because so many small-cap companies are serial capital-raisers, institutional investors spend considerable amounts of time assessing how effectively management has deployed financing proceeds historically and also whether management has used capital for the purposes that were set forth when the capital was

raised. In short, institutional investors are smart, they listen carefully, and they take good notes. Therefore, the **key point** for directors here is to have a keen understanding of how well the company has performed in this regard, since it will frame the company's ability to garner additional capital, and it will impact the associated dilution.

9. *Be realistic about applicable corporate bylaws, exchange rules, and state and federal regulations.* Among the biggest challenges for small-cap officers and directors is that their diminutive, thinly capitalized, and leanly staffed companies are subject to the same rubric of rules and regulations as multi-billion dollar public companies. And, to make matters worse, small-cap companies typically lack the extensive in-house legal teams found at most Fortune 500 companies. Therefore, and especially in advance of any type of financing, officers and directors of small-cap companies need to work together with counsel and auditors to determine whether there are any bylaws, exchange rules, or state and federal regulations which will have an impact on a company's impending financing plans. Though the preparation in this regard should be relatively straightforward, the failure to undertake these analyses thoroughly and in a timely manner is easily one of the most recurring impediments to successful financings. The **key point** here is to start well in advance of every financing and make sure that officers and directors are satisfied that all systems are go prior to taking any more steps. Literally dozens of small-cap financings are scuttled every year (some with disastrous consequences) because officers and directors are alerted at the last second that the company, for example, has insufficient authorized shares, the share class envisioned by the financing isn't authorized by the company, the exchange's rules forbid the size of the financing because of the company's market capitalization, the company is

forbidden from selling shares in a particular state because of unheeded state securities regulations (i.e., Blue Sky laws), or the company can't utilize an otherwise effective registration statement because of a failure to include a particular class of securities. Regrettably, the list goes on and on. The good news, however, is that these problems are completely preventable with appropriate organization and forethought.

10. *Be realistic about what type of investors own the company's stock.* By and large, the vast majority of mid- and large-cap companies are owned by mutual funds and hedge funds, with retail investors occupying the remaining 10 to 15 percent or less. The ownership of small-cap companies varies dramatically by market capitalization with some of the smallest public companies completely lacking in institutional ownership. There are numerous reasons why institutional investors steer clear of small-cap companies: some are foreclosed by mandate; others can't invest unless a company has at least a $5 or $10 stock price or a $250 million market capitalization; others can't invest in companies that aren't listed on major exchanges; and still others are functionally foreclosed on a case-by-case basis because there is simply too little liquidity to be able to build a base position without unduly influencing the stock price to go higher. The **key point** here is that regardless of the reasons why a stock is owned by some and not by others, officers and directors need to collectively understand what types of investors own their stock especially in advance of a financing. The reasons are simple: an astonishing amount of time and money is wasted by many small-cap companies either pursuing investors that literally or figuratively can't buy the stock being offered, or pursuing investors without first committing any thought to what those investors do for a living.

Being brutally realistic is a great starting point for small-cap directors and will better position the board to constructively begin the financing process. In the chapters of Part One, each aspect of the corporate finance process is reviewed chronologically along with key points for boards to analyze and common mistakes to avoid.

CHAPTER 1

START EVERY FINANCING WITH THE SAME THREE-STEP PROCESS

Three Steps to Start Every Financing

Key considerations for directors:

- *Step one*: Assessing of gating issues which can immediately impact a company's financing plans.

- *Step two*: Determining how much capital the company should try to raise is part art and part science.

- *Step three*: The use of proceeds can impact what type of financing is possible.

Common mistakes to avoid:

- Boards often outsource or delay vetting the pertinent "gotchas" to the detriment of shareholders.

- Boards need to confirm that the counsel being used by management are qualified corporate finance lawyers.

- Boards need to focus more on what is "possible" and less on what is "needed."

- Boards often fail to think through how investors view the reasons why the company is raising capital.

B y far the most common shortcoming in the way small-cap boards often approach a financing is the failure to begin by thoroughly and systematically vetting the factors, both inside and outside the company, that could materially impact how much money can be raised, when, and on what terms— the "gotchas." It is in the nature of gotchas that some are intuitive and in plain sight, while others are convoluted and obtuse. One thing is clear—boards that don't ask the pertinent questions in the formative stages of a financing and then have a replicable process for assimilating the answers risk unnecessary dilution.

GOTCHAS COME IN MANY SHAPES AND SIZES

Prior to delving into the three-step process, it would be helpful first to provide some context concerning how otherwise one-dimensional factors can coalesce under various circumstances to impact a company's ability to raise capital:

1. *Market data and deal lawyers.* Company ABC decides that it is going to file a Form S-3 registration statement. Upon it being declared effective by the Securities and Exchange Commission, the company will attempt to raise capital by selling registered common stock to investors. In its zeal to get the registration statement ("shelf") filed, ABC's board doesn't do any analysis of recent shelf offerings that were undertaken by companies like ABC. Moreover, one of ABC's directors is an outspoken critic of warrants and convinces the rest of ABC's board that the shelf registration should be limited to common stock only (i.e., no warrants). ABC's outside counsel, though from a large law firm, doesn't have much experience with small-cap finance and simply goes along with the wishes of the board.

The SEC undertakes a full review of the S-3, and it's not declared effective for three months, during which time ABC's cash reserves have diminished considerably. Once the S-3 is declared effective, members of ABC's management meet with several bankers to decide which firm is best suited to assist with the raising of capital. Each of the banks, in turn, informs ABC that it can't raise capital for ABC because institutional investors won't consider investing in ABC unless ABC also offers warrants with underlying registered common stock. Upon consultation with counsel, ABC is informed that the S-3 can't be amended to add warrants and would need to be completely refiled. In order not to run out of money completely, ABC is forced to sell stock at a 50 percent greater discount to its closing bid price than other comparable companies have done recently in order to make up for the fact that it couldn't offer warrants. The **key point** here is that had the members of ABC's board taken the time first to review the terms of registered offerings recently completed by similar companies prior to filing the registration statement, they would have seen that every one of those financings included warrants, an outspoken board member's preference notwithstanding. Moreover, if ABC had hired deal lawyers with substantive experience in small-cap finance, that attorney likely would have advised ABC to file a universal shelf registration (which includes multiple different kinds of securities, and affords companies maximum flexibility without needing to refile).

2. *Prior company financings.* Last year, Company DEF sold convertible notes with warrants to investors. Among other things, the warrants provided that they were exercisable into DEF's common stock at $5.00 per share if certain conditions were met. The warrants also contained a provision that stated

that if DEF were to sell any stock to investors while the warrants were still outstanding for a price that was lower than $5.00, then the exercise price of the warrants would reset to the lower price (this type of provision is quite common in small-cap finance and is commonly referred to as "price protection" or "full ratchet antidilution"). Upon closer inspection though, the antidilution went a step further and provided that in addition to resetting the exercise price of the warrants, DEF also had to issue those investors more warrants so that they could maintain the benefit of their prior deal (also known as "exploding warrants"). Subsequent to the convertible note financing, DEF's business had dealt with numerous challenges, it had only six months of operating capital remaining, and its stock price had fallen to $2.00. In anticipation of a new financing, the board and counsel confirmed that, though quite dilutive, the company had sufficient authorized shares to raise enough capital to provide four quarters of operating runway to turn things around. Then counsel for a prospective institutional investor established that the envisioned financing would trigger the warrant's antidilution mechanism since it would be transacted at a price under $5.00, and it would also trigger the exploding warrants. Consequently, DEF would not have sufficient authorized shares to issue to the warrant holders and the new investors: DEF would either breach the convertible note (by not issuing authorized shares to the warrant holders) and make it immediately due, or the company will have to delay the offering in order to solicit shareholder approval (which may or may not be forthcoming) to increase the authorized share count. The **key point** here is that, as is unfortunately quite common, many structured financings are challenging to understand even for experienced lawyers, much less nonlawyers. The complexity of these instruments is further compounded by members of the management team failing to carefully review them or failing to have them reviewed for the board in sufficient detail in advance of a financing.

3. *Regulations and timing.* Company GHI is running out of capital, and its senior secured lender is unwilling to give the company more room on the outstanding facility. GHI requests that the lender waive the prohibition against adding any subordinated debt, but the lender refuses. GHI's board approaches some of the company's existing investors and asks whether any of them would be inclined to invest further capital in the company in exchange for equity. Unfortunately, as GHI's fortunes have diminished, so has the average daily volume in GHI's stock. Therefore, existing investors are hesitant to invest a large amount of money in exchange for common stock because they fear that the trading volume is insufficient to support an exit should they want one. After looking outside the company unsuccessfully, GHI reapproaches its existing investors. The investors give GHI's board a choice of accepting a smaller investment in exchange for common stock, or they will consider providing the total amount the board has requested in the form of a convertible preferred instrument (i.e.; the thinking being that since further debt is contractually forbidden, perhaps the investors can mitigate their downside by collecting a dividend while they wait for GHI's fortunes to improve, and the preferred stock shouldn't be a problem for the lenders). GHI's board likes the idea of getting all the capital at once and proceeds to negotiate the terms of the convertible preferred instrument with the existing investors for nearly a month. Since GHI doesn't have in-house counsel, GHI's board negotiates the lion's share of the terms prior to getting outside counsel involved. When outside counsel reviews the terms the

parties have agreed to, the attorneys explain to the board that because of how the preferred instrument is structured, the SEC would actually consider the preferred stock to be debt on GHI's balance sheet,[2] thus violating the lender's covenant. With GHI's back firmly against the wall, the board agrees to the smaller common stock financing previously proposed, but on far worse terms given the passage of time and GHI's dire situation. The **key point** here is that since so many small-cap companies operate without in-house counsel, directors need to take steps to address any potentially gating issues at the formative stages of the board's finance planning because time is rarely on the side of small-cap companies that require financing.

These few examples are not intended to be comprehensive but are intended to illustrate that gating issues abound in small-cap finance, and it's better to have a process to ferret them out sooner rather than later.

TIP

Almost as damaging to a small-cap company's financing efforts as ignoring all the various possible impediments to a successful financing is analyzing them in an illogical order. That is, in much the same way that it's ill-advised to frame a house and then perform a soil analysis, it also doesn't make sense for a board to determine how much capital it needs, hire a banker, and then run through a checklist of possible problems prior to closing the financing. Just as a soil analysis informs the builder as to what type of house is possible to build on a particular site, a thorough preliminary analysis of gating factors helps dictate not only what type of financing is actually possible, but also what type of banking firm can be most helpful. Unfortunately, small-cap boards often "build first, and ask questions later."

STEP ONE: ANALYZING THE GATING ISSUES

Legal: Immediately after making a preliminary decision to raise capital, directors need to ensure that management and counsel are focused on some of the legal issues[3] that can alter or stop even the best-conceived financing plans:

- *How many shares can be issued?* Senior U.S. stock exchanges (e.g., NYSE, NYSE MKT, and Nasdaq) all prohibit the issuance of more than a prescribed percentage of the issued and outstanding shares of a stock if those shares are going to be sold in a privately negotiated transaction[4] at a discount to the market price or book value (whichever is greater), unless companies first receive shareholder approval. For Nasdaq-listed companies, this is typically referred to as the "20 percent rule," since that is the prescribed percentage. It's critical for counsel to be clear with officers and directors concerning exactly how many shares may be issued, because failure to abide by these marketplaces rules subjects the company to being delisted. If the company is not listed on a senior exchange, the prohibitions on how many shares may be issued without prior shareholder approval are likely less restrictive; it's equally important to get clarity on this issue from counsel.

- *What kinds of shares are authorized and in what numbers?* Every small-cap finance veteran has at least a dozen stories about companies that got all the way to the end of a financing only to realize that either a certain class of stock wasn't authorized by its articles of incorporation or that the class of stock was authorized but there were an insufficient number of shares remaining to be issued without a shareholder vote. Accordingly, directors should make sure that counsel has reviewed these issue before they proceed.

- *What kind of stock does the company envision selling?*

  - *Restricted stock.* Directors should be aware that Rule 144 was amended in 2008. It's important to make sure that counsel informs the officers and directors of what holding periods will likely apply to investors who purchase restricted stock from the company.

  - *Restricted stock with registration rights.* It's important for counsel to advise the officers and directors of what type of resale registration statement the company is eligible to utilize and what restrictions, if any, exist on the number of shares it can register at one time.

  - *Registered stock.* In light of amendments made to the eligibility requirements for registration statements on Form S-3 in 2008, it's important for counsel to let the officers and directors know whether the company is S-3 eligible,[5] and if it is, whether there is a limit on how many shares may be sold.

- *Will the debt or equity to be issued violate any agreements or trigger any covenants?*

  - *Banking.* Is the company obligated to utilize a certain investment bank in accordance with a prior banking agreement?

  - *Investors.* Are there investors who have a contractual right of first refusal or right of participation in any subsequent equity or debt financing?

  - *Breach.* Will a debt or equity offering breach the terms of any existing company obligation, or in the case of debt will an intercreditor agreement be required?

  - *Antidilution.* Will an equity or equity-linked offering trigger any contractual antidilution provisions that will reset outstanding instruments lower?

TIP

Addressing legal issues that arise out of small-cap corporate finance presupposes that companies have qualified counsel assisting them. Unfortunately, this is sometimes not the case for one primary reason: deal lawyers are too often selected because of an existing relationship rather than because they possess the requisite experience. While existing company counsel might well be perfectly qualified, it's important for directors to keep in mind that lawyers either have extensive, recent, highly relevant small-cap corporate finance experience, or they don't. Especially since so many small-cap companies operate without in-house counsel, the need to have experienced deal lawyers can't be overemphasized. Accordingly, directors should confirm with management that the actual attorney (i.e., not the firm, but the actual attorney) working on the financing has counseled at least a handful of substantially similar companies in the previous six to twelve months in connection with the same type of financing the company intends to transact. If there is one thing officers and directors should be sure of, it's that the hedge funds that are investing in the company definitely have those lawyers (and then some).

After addressing some of the most important legal issues, the officers and directors will be armed with a framework for what is possible. With respect to a possible equity offering, they have confirmed how many shares they might be able to issue, what kind of shares they can issue, whether and to what extent they might be able to offer restricted stock (with or without registration rights) or fully registered stock, and whether and to what extent a stock issuance will affect other company obligations. With respect to a possible debt offering, they have confirmed how such a debt offering might impact existing contractual obligations.

Time: The other preliminary variable for the board to consider is time.
Does the company have any latitude with respect to the timing of the
financing, or does the company need the capital infusion as quickly as
possible:

- *Time is of the essence.* Best plans and intentions notwithstanding,
  small-cap companies often require infusions of capital as soon as
  commercially practicable. And unlike private companies that might
  find themselves in similar circumstances, when public companies
  are in need of capital quickly, everyone knows. Consequently,
  when time is of the essence, small-cap companies have fewer
  financing alternatives. For example:(1) unless a company in need
  of quick financing already has an effective registration statement,
  it's unlikely to be able to risk the time needed to draft and file a
  registration statement (and wait for it to be declared effective by
  the SEC) in order to sell registered primary shares; and (2) it's
  often challenging for small-cap companies with their backs up
  against the wall to secure institutional loans given the frequent lack
  of material cash flow and fixed assets. The **key point** here is that
  when raising capital is not elective, boards need to quickly focus
  on the types of financing that are the likeliest to be obtained; for
  example, for small-cap companies that need capital quickly (and
  don't already have an effective registration statement available), a
  private placement of restricted stock or debt is often the most likely
  scenario. For companies that have effective registration statements
  available, a privately negotiated shelf takedown is often the most
  likely scenario.[6]

- *Timing is flexible.* Subject to the legal issues discussed earlier,
  greater time flexibility can provide small-cap companies with
  more financing alternatives. For example, more time can permit
  registration statements to be prepared, reviewed, and be declared
  effective; in addition the company could be able to make public

offerings of stock, contemplate strategic financings, and consider commercial credit facilities.[7] Moreover, more time can provide officers and directors with the ability to time a financing to coincide with compelling macro or company events, or take advantage of market or industry dynamics.

TIP

Small-cap directors routinely get frustrated by what they view as anomalous financing results. That is, a peer company that isn't per-forming well, and very nearly ran out of money is able to undertake a less dilutive financing than the company that by most objective measures is not only performing better but also has the luxury of having more time resulting from more prudent financial planning. This is a uniquely small-cap phenomenon and is highly dependent on two variables. In order of importance they are trading volume and management dynamism. Simply put, a small-cap company that is running on fumes but has a liquid stock and a dynamic manage-ment team can often attract less dilutive financing terms than a better-performing company with less liquid stock and a less impres-sive management team. Directors approaching a financing need to be mindful of the fact that for small-cap investors, liquidity is of paramount importance for a simple reason—risks are ubiquitous in the small-cap ecosystem, and trading volume enables investors to exit with more of their capital than less if fortune doesn't shine on a given investment. Accordingly, as officers and directors prepare for a financing, they should remind each other of the small-cap investor's mantra: "It's better to be liquid than good!"

After discussing the gating issues of time and applicable regulations/laws, directors can analyze how those issues impact the amount of capital the company seeks to raise.

STEP TWO: HOW MUCH CAPITAL?

A common mistake made by small-cap officers and directors is contemplating capital needs with too much emphasis on what is "desired" versus what is "realistic." Prior to discussing a more advantageous way for boards to arrive at the amount of capital they need, it's worth elaborating on why this mistake happens so regularly.

First, as experienced small-cap institutional investors will attest, there is an entitlement ethos that thrives in the small-cap ecosystem when it comes to growth capital. Many management teams and boards willingly or subconsciously adopt a mindset that suggests that somehow a ticker symbol equals the right to capital.[8] Reasonable people differ about why this viewpoint exists. Perhaps it's a result of officers and board members being serially conditioned by professional service providers to believe that one of the principal reasons why companies put up with austere costs and regulations of being publicly traded is that there is a benefit that private companies don't have—easier access to capital. Regardless of the cause, the damaging effect that this mindset can have on officers and directors is when capital needs are determined predominantly by "head-in-the-sand" budgeting; for example, "The operating plan dictates that in order to take the next step toward building the company into a multi-billion dollar industry leader, the company absolutely needs to raise $X."

Second, the entitlement ethos can be further enabled by boards that don't first focus on the gating issues that might impact how much capital they can actually raise.

Boards should consider the following three-step approach in determining the amount of capital to be raised:

- *What are the nonmarket financing limitations?* Given the gating issues previously discussed, the directors, assisted by counsel, should first determine the legal, regulatory, and temporal limits, if any, on the amount of money that the company can raise.

- *What are the market-based financing limitations?* Beyond legal and regulatory impediments, statistical undercurrents are pervasive in small-cap finance. That is, if the board does some research into private placements of debt and equity and public offerings transacted by other companies of similar size, industry, trading volume, and so on, it will become clear how much capital investors are willing to invest as a percentage of market capitalization or daily trading volume. As is discussed in more detail in Chapter 2, these data are critical to digest, inasmuch as they can be instructive concerning the amount of capital that can be raised and with what type of structure.[9] The **key point** here is that rather than outsourcing this research to others and/or doing it much later in the financing process, small-cap boards need to take advantage of the ease with which this research can be done[10] and understand that the time to do it is in the formative stages of contemplating a financing.

- *Balancing reality with operational needs.* After determining what's possible and then what's likely, the officers and directors need to balance those results with the company's operational needs. If the operational needs of the business exceed what's either possible or likely, then the officers and the directors (along with counsel)[11] need to determine whether and to what extent the funding needs of the company can be accomplished through a series of financings instead of just one. If the operational needs of the business fall below what's possible and likely, then the board can either proceed toward raising that amount of capital or, if there is time and macro/ micro sentiment permits, the board can weigh whether it would be prudent to raise a bit more capital than is currently required—in other words, opportunistically strengthen the balance sheet.

TIP

When arriving at a preliminary determination of how much capital to raise, boards should try to resist the temptation of becoming fixated on raising a particular sum and instead think in terms of ranges. A range of capital provides the board with the flexibility to either raise or lower the amount of capital depending upon dilution. A range also provides investors with the same flexibility. However, ranges that are too broad (i.e., greater than 35–40 percent) can suggest indecision or desperation.

After determining the preliminary range of capital to be raised, the board needs to be clear about what the capital will be used for and mindful of the fact that the stated use of proceeds can itself affect how much money can realistically be raised.

STEP THREE: THE USE OF PROCEEDS

Because small-cap companies often raise money many times while they're on their respective paths to mid-cap life and beyond, their credibility with institutional investors is inextricably linked to how well they've driven value subsequent to prior financings. Simply put, there are some small-cap companies that use new growth capital as promised and create demonstrable value for the shareholders in the process, and there are other small-cap companies that do varying degrees of the opposite. It's vital for the board to be brutally realistic about the company's track record in this regard, because it will likely impact the terms, structure, and amount of capital that can be raised. Also the board should be mindful that the stated use of proceeds can affect the amount of money that can be raised. Broadly speaking, there are three common uses of capital in the small-cap ecosystem:

- *General corporate purposes.* The most common use of proceeds is for general corporate purposes. This is essentially catch-all nomenclature that refers to things like normalizing accounts payable, hiring, technology purchases, clinical trial advancement, facilities improvement, and so on. Since it's the most normally stated reason for raising capital, this use of proceeds is rarely impactful, in and of itself, on a prospective financing.

TIP

Although it may be self-evident, companies should not signal to investors that proceeds will be used for general corporate purposes if in fact they aren't to be used for that purpose. Boards need to be mindful of the fact that in the small-cap ecosystem "general corporate purposes" does not equal: launching/funding expensive patent litigation against a large-cap company, buying back the company's stock, making investments in other companies, or spending the lion's share of the funding on several Super Bowl ads. This happens much more often than one would imagine, and the results are predictable—for example, future capital is either nonexistent or a lot more expensive. Therefore, boards should make sure that management is clear about the uses and then monitor the uses.

- *Debt repayment.* Although repayment of debt is certainly a valid use of proceeds, boards need to understand that small-cap investors tend to frown on this. To many investors, the repayment of debt suggests stasis rather than growth; for example, instead of hiring new people, putting new production lines in the factory, or advancing a drug closer to commercialization (i.e., all things that could provide growth and stock appreciation), the company is improving its balance sheet (i.e., something less likely to provide stock appreciation in the nearer term). This matters because investor reticence can materially alter terms, structure, and the amount of capital that can be raised. The **key point** here is that if boards feel that raising capital for the principal purpose of repaying debt is prudent for the shareholders, they should also consider raising a small amount of money simultaneously for general corporate purposes in order to add to the attractiveness of the financing.

- *Acquisition financing.* Raising capital to purchase the assets or stock of another entity presents unique challenges in the small-cap ecosystem for two principal reasons: (1) many small-cap companies can't afford to hire expert consultants to assist in valuing assets and stock; and (2) many small-cap management teams have limited experience in acquiring and integrating assets or companies. Because small-cap investors are conspicuously aware of these issues, the **key point** here is that boards need to be aware that the terms, structure, and amount of capital they can garner may be affected by this intended use of proceeds.

TIP

Boards should note that small-cap acquisition financing often takes the form of a private placement that is announced simultaneously with the acquisition. Private placements are often conducive to acquisition financing because investors are already in possession of material, non-public information (i.e., the company's intent to undertake a private placement) and restricted from trading during which time they can also learn about the details of the acquisition. Small-cap investors tend to prefer this scenario, because they have the opportunity to profit from any post-announcement stock price appreciation. This arbitrage opportunity is obviated if the acquisition is announced first, and financing is sought after.

Through systematically vetting the most pertinent factors than can impact a financing, this three-step process provides boards with a framework for realistically assessing how much capital they might be able to raise. The next step is for the board to preliminarily analyze what structure is not only possible but the most likely.

Notes

1. The term "small-cap" as used in this book includes, by reference, small-cap, micro-cap, and nano-cap companies.

2. This is a function of Financial Accounting Standards Board ("FASB") Statement of Financial Accounting Standard No. 150.

3. This is not intended to be an exhaustive, detailed discussion of the laws associated with corporate finance. Rather, the purpose of these lists is to inform directors of important issues and suggest that companies and counsel consider them in conjunction with their existing protocols. Directors needn't undergo an immersion law course in order to make sure that these issues are addressed and that they are addressed early in the financing process. For a considerably more detailed analysis of all the relevant laws associated with small-cap finance, see, for example, Steven Dresner, The Issuer's Guide to PIPEs (New York: Bloomberg Press, 2009), pp. 97–120.

4. These prohibitions don't apply to public offerings.

5. There are two basic ways that issuers can register primary shares (vs. resale shares) with the SEC. The first is with Form S-1; the second is with Form S-3. Form S-3 is typically cheaper and more company friendly because it permits issuers to incorporate all its prior Exchange Act filings and future one's by reference automatically without the need to refile each time information is updated. It also enables companies to opportunistically sell shares from time to time when it's most beneficial for them to do so. Accordingly, in most cases companies would likely utilize Form S-3 to register primary shares if they are eligible.

6. All the common small-cap financing structures are covered in depth in Chapter 2, in addition to less common situations like "Well-Known Seasoned Issuer" ("WKSI") filers.

7. It's important for directors to avoid a common misconception, which is that just because a small-cap company has the time and is able to possibly execute, for example, a registered or public offering, doesn't mean that those terms will necessarily be less dilutive than what the same company could achieve by undertaking a private placement. In short, more alternatives don't necessarily equate to less dilutive.

8. This mindset has certainly evolved given the dearth of growth capital availability in the wake of the current financial crisis. Subsequent to previous downturns, the same comportment has proved resilient.

9. To directors who are more familiar with larger public companies, this is an understandably alien concept. But it's important to remember that many small-cap companies are not only nascent and cash-flow negative, but they are also not followed by equity research analysts and have illiquid stocks. Therefore, rather than being valued independently based upon earnings or free cash flow, the default setting in small-cap finance is that companies are often constrained by the amounts of capital raised and the structures used by other companies with similar capital markets profiles.

10. Whether it's accessing proprietary capital markets databases like PrivateRaise, Dealogic, Knobias, PlacementTracker, or Capital IQ (or a combination of all five), officers and directors can pay nominal amounts of money to access the same proprietary databases that investment bankers and institutional investors use.

11. The reason why involving counsel in this analysis is important is that under certain circumstances, subsequent financings that are similar in structure with similar investors could become integrated and be considered one transaction for purposes of applicable laws/regulations.

CHAPTER 2

SELECTING A
FINANCING STRUCTURE

Optimal Structure Versus What's Most Likely

Key considerations for directors:

- Make sure the board is apprised of the pros and cons of the most frequently utilized small-cap financing structures.
- When contemplating convertible instruments and warrants, make sure the company's auditors have relevant experience with unique accounting issues, and involve them in the formative discussions.
- The distinctions between RDs, CMPOs, and follow-ons are critical for boards to master.
- Many small-cap companies can't avoid issuing warrants, but they can take steps to mitigate the impact of warrants.
- Boards need to consider multiple factors when determining the optimal financing structure. Making the determinations is not always intuitive.

- The "optimal" structure needs to be juxtaposed against the "most likely" structure.

Common mistakes to avoid:

- If you decide to defer to a board member's corporate finance acumen, make sure the deference is deserved.
- By failing to think like institutional investors, many small-cap directors remain mired in misconceptions about different financing structures.
- Small-cap boards routinely outsource critical corporate finance decisions to conflicted third-parties instead of making their own informed decisions utilizing highly instructive data.

F ew small-cap boards channel Charles Darwin during discussions regarding which structure is most apt for a prospective financing—but they should. Once a board analyzes what type of financing might be possible, how much money it needs, and what purposes it will use the financing for (e.g., the preliminary analyses discussed in Chapter 1), all these elements next must coalesce into a determination of the financing structure that will be optimal for the company. The strongest, most actively traded companies often can transact the type of financing that is best suited for them. For smaller, less liquid companies the financing structure is often dictated to them by investors, regardless of board preferences. This Darwinist continuum isn't sufficiently appreciated by small-cap directors and thus leads to lost time, lost opportunities, and misunderstandings.

In order for boards to realistically assess financing structure, they need to be conversant with the menu of frequently utilized structures, then determine what type of financing structure is optimal for the company, and, perhaps most importantly, study what financing structure is also the most likely for the company given its size and capital markets profile.

FREQUENTLY UTILIZED STRUCTURES

Because small-cap boards frequently do not have corporate finance and capital markets experts on them, there are often material misunderstandings about the basic pros and cons of the most frequently utilized small-cap financing structures. Below is a list of basic financing structures (and associated pros and cons) from the most often utilized to the least in the small-cap ecosystem.[1]

TIP

While it's very common for small-cap boards not to have any corporate finance or capital markets experts, small-cap directors need to guard against another recurring scenario that is arguably worse than not having any board expertise at all in this regard. It's quite common for small-cap directors to defer to the one board member who appears to have the most corporate finance and capital markets experience. Such deference is not always justified. There isn't a small-cap banker or institutional investor who doesn't have multiple horror stories about the small-cap board that deferred all finance and capital markets decision making to a director who was a highly successful bond trader at Salomon Brothers in the 1980s (but who knew virtually nothing about small-cap finance) only to flirt with or succumb to bankruptcy as a result. The **key point** for directors is to remember that just because a board member has some finance or capital markets experience *doesn't necessarily mean that this person is knowledgeable about the highly specific nuances of financing a small-cap company in today's market*. Moreover, the board should be similarly cautious when a director expresses reticence with respect to a particular financing structure in the absence of objective data.

RESTRICTED COMMON STOCK

By an order of magnitude of three to four times in some years, the most common financing structure employed by small-cap companies is restricted common stock. More specifically, this involves the sale of authorized, newly issued shares of unregistered common stock to accredited investors subsequent to a privately negotiated, confidential transaction. It is referred to as "restricted" common stock because it is ineligible for resale on an exchange until it's either registered or all the conditions for resale under Rule 144 are satisfied. Depending upon the agreement reached between the investors and the company, the shares carry registration rights (which require the company to take steps within a prescribed time period to include the shares in a resale registration statement) or the shares lack registration rights and become salable in due course subject to the provisions of Rule 144.[2]

Pros

- *Speed to market.* Because restricted common stock is sold prior to undertaking the registration process with the SEC, companies can transact a financing in as little as several weeks. Consequently, companies are better able to take advantage of strength in the market or other events.

- *Lower transactional expenses.* Inasmuch as the sale of restricted common stock is the least complex form of financing, it typically results in a lower transactional expense (especially if the restricted stock doesn't have registration rights).

- *Simplicity.* From a balance sheet perspective as well as from a "Street" perspective, common stock is easily understood.

Cons

- *Pricing.* Because investors are purchasing stock that is ineligible for immediate or even near-term resale, unregistered common stock is regularly issued at a meaningful discount to the closing bid price or the volume-weighted average price (VWAP). Discounts of 20 percent, for example, are not uncommon.

- *Registration restrictions and penalties.* Directors need to make sure that management is working closely with experienced counsel to ensure that the company is not attempting to register more shares than are permitted by applicable exchange rules and securities regulations. Additionally, directors need to make sure that the company is able to satisfy the negotiated registration timetable, if any, since penalties for breaching the schedule can be onerous.

- *Hedging.* Because investors are purchasing stock that is ineligible for immediate or even near-term resale, investors in the transaction, where practicable, might sell the same or substantially similar number of shares acquired in the financing short after the financing is announced in order to attempt to lock-in the negotiated discount.[3] If this is done, it can negatively affect the stock price. Moreover, since this practice is widely known and expected, even investors who didn't participate in the restricted common stock financing might seek to sell the stock short or simply sell their stock to either take advantage of the likely fall in the stock price or avoid it.

- *Offering size limitation.* All the senior exchanges in the United States have rules that require shareholder approval prior to closing any privately negotiated offerings where the company seeks to sell a certain percentage (typically 20 percent) of the company's issued and outstanding stock at a discount to the closing bid price.

TIP

Small-cap directors often get fixated on whether hedge funds might short their stock in connection with a financing. When they become fixated in this way, they can't see the forest for the trees. Though this is discussed in greater detail in Part Two, it's important for directors to keep in mind that finance, especially small-cap finance, is about trade-offs. That is, companies seek to garner growth capital with the least dilution possible, while investors seek to maximize their upside and minimize their downside. The stronger the company, the more the balance inures to its benefit; and the weaker the company, the more the balance shifts to the investors. As it pertains particularly to restricted common stock financings, directors need to be brutally realistic about what is being transacted—the company is getting its money in the near term, while the investors can't sell their stock for an appreciable period of time, company performance and stock market notwithstanding. Accordingly, the investors shouldn't be vilified for attempting to lawfully maximize the benefit of their bargain. Instead, management and directors should simply assume that if the stock is sufficiently liquid and the shares of the company are borrowable, then investors in the financing might seek to *hedge* their positions. Lest any director think that investors are not going to do so, it's worth reiterating that they are called hedge funds for a reason. If a company would like to minimize its risk, then it should take the time and spend the money to register the stock first (i.e., there is no reason for investors in a financing to short the company's stock if they are issued registered shares that are immediately eligible for resale after the transaction is announced). The **key point** here is that management and boards contemplating a restricted common stock offering should focus on the benefits and then strive to put the capital to great use so that the company can be in a better bargaining position if and when it needs to raise capital again.

Registered Common Stock (Fully Marketed Follow-on Offering)

A follow-on offering is functionally the same as an IPO except that the company's stock is already publicly traded. Therefore, a follow-on differs from a restricted common stock financing in several important ways. First, while the shares being sold are also authorized, newly issued shares of common stock (as in a restricted common stock financing), follow-on shares are already registered so that investors in the financing are free to resell the shares on whatever exchange the company's shares trade after the financing is transacted and announced. Second, the intent to undertake a follow-on offering is announced first and publicly marketed thereafter, while the intent to undertake a restricted common stock offering is not publicly announced, is privately negotiated, and is announced only after the financing is consummated. Last, a follow-on offering is fully underwritten by investment banks, while a restricted stock offering isn't.

Pros

- *Ability to market/showcase company's strengths.* Because follow-on offerings are announced publicly, there is an opportunity to communicate the company's story and strategy to a broad audience of new prospective investors.

- *Greater flexibility on offering size.* All the senior exchanges in the United States have rules that require shareholder approval prior to any privately negotiated offerings where the company seeks to sell a certain percentage (typically 20 percent) of the company's issued and outstanding stock at a discount to the closing bid price. Since follow-on offerings are publicly announced prior to being transacted, no such shareholder approval is required.

- *Equity research.* Although investment banking and equity research are always independent functions, most investment banks wouldn't consider underwriting a follow-on offering unless their equity research analyst was intent on initiating research coverage of the stock. Therefore, companies that transact follow-on offerings often are able to add to their existing equity research base and leverage new institutional sales forces.

- *Underwritten.* Follow-on offerings are fully underwritten, which means that once the investment banks present the terms of the financing to the company on the night of pricing and the terms are accepted, there is very little risk that the company will not get the funds.

- *Simplicity.* From a balance sheet perspective as well as from a "Street" perspective, common stock is easily understood.

Cons

- *Market risk (double discount).* Because follow-on offerings are publicly announced, and then transacted, there is material risk that the stock price will drop when the financing is announced because of the impending dilution. After the initial announcement, the financing is often priced at a discount to wherever the stock stabilizes after the announcement. Therefore, companies can, in some sense, be subject to a "double discount" when undertaking a follow-on offering.

- *Time and focus.* Selecting and negotiating an underwriting syndicate can take appreciable time. Moreover, during the marketing roadshow of a follow-on offering, management might visit numerous cities (and sometimes travel abroad) for up to seven days. The time (which is in addition to the registration statement being drafted and subsequently declared effective by the SEC) and lost focus on the business can be material. Follow-ons are not well suited to companies that require capital quickly.

TIP

Notwithstanding the fact that follow-on offerings are quite common in the small-cap ecosystem, many small-cap directors have never participated in a follow-on offering. Therefore, the nomenclature, responsibilities, and fees are not well understood. Simply put, when it comes to syndicate roles in a follow-on offering, investment banks occupy one of two roles—bookrunners or comanagers. Bookrunners are responsible for executing the transaction (drafting, positioning, marketing, pricing, and allocation). The "lead left" bookrunner essentially shepherds the execution of the transaction and is also typically responsible for postdeal price stabilization (i.e., the over allotment). The "right" bookrunner is similarly responsible for execution, but is somewhat subservient to the lead left bookrunner's intradeal judgment calls and typically isn't responsible for postdeal stabilization. It's most common in a small-cap follow-on to have two or three bookrunners. The other nonbookrunning investment banks are referred to as comanagers.

Comanagers don't have execution responsibilities per se, but assist with marketing and otherwise support the financing. Typically, the bookrunners divide 75 to 80 percent of the overall fees, and comanagers split the remaining 20 to 25 percent. Though there are certainly exceptions, the typical investment banking fee for a small-cap follow-on is 5 to 6 percent of the gross proceeds. Sometimes, 1 percent of the deal fee will be presented as an optional incentive fee if the company feels that the bankers have performed above and beyond expectations.

Convertible Preferred Stock

In the small-cap realm, convertible instruments allow accredited investors to acquire common shares at a negotiated price by converting or exchanging another security. In the case of convertible preferred stock, investors typically have the choice of retaining preferred stock (along with a dividend paid in cash, common stock, or more convertible preferred and liquidation priority), or converting the preferred stock into common stock. Typically, the common stock underlying the convertible preferred is restricted at the time of issuance but has registration rights. Like a restricted common stock offering, this structure is typically privately negotiated.

Pros

- *Balance sheet.* If structured properly, convertible preferred stock can appear on the balance sheet as equity.

- *Pricing.* Unlike restricted common stock, convertible preferred stock typically has less discounted pricing and might even convert at market (when issued) or at a premium to market (when issued).[4]

- *Structure.* Although commonly viewed as a negative by boards, being able to structure the terms of a convertible preferred instrument to complement the company's needs and situation can be a benefit if artfully negotiated.

Cons [5]

- *Structure.* Although structure can be a positive under some circumstances, it can certainly also impose restraints on operating the business in the form of ongoing covenants and dividend payments. Moreover, the optics of a structured instrument can deter otherwise interested prospective investors.

- *Process.* A company must be authorized to issue preferred stock and also likely needs to file a certificate of designation for the preferred stock with the secretary of state in the state of incorporation. If the company is not authorized to issue preferred stock, it would likely require shareholder approval to amend the company's articles of incorporation. Also the payment of dividends is often regulated by corporate laws in the state of incorporation, so directors need to make sure that management and counsel are well-versed in this.

- *Accounting.* Convertible instruments typically contain embedded derivatives which require special accounting treatment. Officers and directors need to make sure that the company's auditors are experienced with this.

- *Offering size.* All the senior exchanges in the United States have rules that require shareholder approval prior to any privately negotiated offerings where the company seeks to sell a certain percentage (typically 20 percent) of the company's issued and outstanding stock at a discount to the closing bid price.

TIP

As alluded to in Chapter 1, there are many small-cap board members who have thought that they were raising equity by transacting a convertible preferred financing only to have federal regulators later reclassify it as debt on the company's balance sheet. In other words, over the course of time many so-called convertible preferred instruments started looking more and more like debt when you read the provisions closely; for example, mandatory redemption features after a specific time. Therefore, the Financial Accounting Standards Board (SFAS No. 150) and the SEC (Rule 5-02.28) promulgated rules that effectively set forth that if convertible preferred instruments look more like debt than equity, then they will be considered such, nomenclature notwithstanding. The **key point** for directors is that when a convertible preferred instrument is being considered, management needs to consult attorneys and auditors *who have first-hand experience in this regard* to determine whether the instrument being considered is likely to be viewed as equity or debt.

CONVERTIBLE NOTE

Like a convertible preferred security, a convertible note allows accredited investors to acquire common shares at a negotiated price by converting or exchanging the note. However, unlike a convertible preferred, a convertible note holder is a creditor of the company. Therefore, the note holder can retain the debt instrument to term (along with interest paid in cash, common stock, or more convertible notes, and a secured or an unsecured position) or convert the note into common stock. Typically, the common stock underlying the convertible note is restricted at the time of issuance but has registration rights. Like a restricted common stock offering, this structure is typically privately negotiated.

Pros

- *Pricing.* Unlike restricted common stock, convertible notes typically have less discounted pricing and might even convert at market (when issued) or at a premium to market (when issued).

- *Structure.* Although commonly viewed as a negative by boards, being able to structure the terms of a convertible note to complement the company's needs and situation can be a benefit if artfully negotiated.

Cons[6]

- *Balance sheet.* Since a convertible note is classified as debt on the balance sheet unless/until converted, it may negatively impact debt to equity ratios.

- *Structure.* Although structure can be a positive under some circumstances, it can certainly also impose restraints on operating the business in the form of ongoing covenants and interest payments. Moreover, the optics of a structured instrument can deter otherwise interested prospective investors.

- *Process.* Since convertible note holders are creditors, notes can be either senior or subordinate to existing debt, and intercreditor negotiations, if necessary, can be contentious, complex, and expensive to document. Moreover, to the extent that a note is secured by corporate collateral, there can be expense and delays associated with valuation and securitization.

- *Accounting.* Convertible instruments typically contain embedded derivatives which require special accounting treatment. Officers and directors need to make sure that the company's auditors are experienced with this.

- *Offering size.* All the senior exchanges in the United States have rules that require shareholder approval prior to any privately negotiated offerings where the company seeks to sell a certain percentage (typically 20 percent) of the company's issued and outstanding stock at a discount to the closing bid price.

TIP

Because there is no formal template for negotiating and transacting convertible notes, there are limitless combinations of provisions that can appear in a given instrument. Though this is covered more extensively in Chapter 5, it's important for management and the board to understand that most of the commonly negotiated convertible note provisions deal with pricing (original issue discounts, fixed and variable price conversion), seniority/collateral (prohibition against future indebtedness), sweeteners (interest make-wholes), downside protection (full-ratchet, weighted average antidilution), liquidity (registration rights, maintaining exchange listings, volume limitations), and risk mitigation (self-liquidating notes, affirmative/negative covenants, buy-ins). The **key point** here is that thinking about these provisions enables officers and directors to avoid the most common mistake in analyzing myriad terms of a convertible note—failing to understand what the investors are trying to achieve with the various provisions. In the same way that cross-border business or political negotiations rely heavily on studying the opposing culture, officers and directors are much better able to negotiate convertible notes, in particular, when they try to think like institutional investors. Last, it also saves precious time and money if the officers and directors review the most recent convertible notes transacted by companies in similar industries with substantially similar capital markets profiles (with particular emphasis on which investors were involved). Since institutional investors tend to use similar term sheets repeatedly and since similar companies often are offered similar terms, it's a great way for the company to know what's likely to be coming its way.

Registered Common Stock (At-The-Market Offering)

At-the-Market offerings (ATMs) are unique financings that are becoming more and more common in the small-cap realm. The most common form[7] of ATMs is public offerings of authorized, newly issued,[8] registered common stock. In ATM offerings the company sells stock directly into the market at its discretion, whenever it wants, through a designated agent at then market prices. More specifically, a company is able to specify timing, minimum price, and volume of all sales under the ATM. Accordingly, ATMs differ materially from follow-on offerings in which a fixed number of shares are sold at one time at a fixed price.

Pros

- *Pricing.* One of the primary benefits of ATMs is that the shares are sold into the natural trading flow of the market (i.e., not discounted) without issuers having to market or announce each recurring ATM sale. Once the registration statement for the ATM shares is declared effective by the SEC, the company can use the ATM opportunistically when the stock is buoyant or trading a lot of volume with minimal impact on the stock price.

- *Flexibility.* Since the timing, size, price, and volume of each ATM sale is controlled by the company, an ATM arguably provides the most flexibility of any commonly used small-cap financing structure.

- *Time/distraction.* Unlike follow-on offerings, no roadshows are required, and limited management time is required for each sale.

- *Cost.* ATM distribution costs typically range from 1 to 3 percent; therefore, they are typically cheaper than most follow-on offerings.

Cons

- *Financing size.* Because the nature of ATMs is to periodically "dribble" registered shares into the market with minimal impact, they are not well suited to companies that require material amounts of capital in one lump sum or in a short period of time.

- *Variable financing cost.* Because ATMs are not sold at fixed prices, the price at which the stock is sold fluctuates with the market. This can be good when the stock price is buoyant and less compelling when the stock price is depressed.

- *Visibility.* Companies with fluctuating, less predictable burn rate visibility aren't good candidates for ATMs because the times they might require capital could be periods when their stock is trading down or is illiquid.

- *Time/registration risk.* Although a company with an effective registration statement can undertake an ATM quickly, a company contemplating an ATM that doesn't yet have an effective registration statement is subject to the vagaries of when the SEC may declare the registration statement effective once drafted and filed. Therefore, companies that need capital quickly shouldn't consider an ATM structure.[9]

REGISTERED COMMON STOCK (EQUITY LINE)

Equity lines are often confused with ATMs, but the two structures are very different. The main difference between them is that unlike an ATM where there are no fixed prices and pricing is agreed upon prior to each drawdown, equity lines rely on fixed prices that are put in place when the equity line agreement is first negotiated between the parties. The most common form of equity line gives the company the unilateral right, subject to negotiated conditions, to compel the investors to buy authorized, newly issued shares of registered common stock at negotiated pricing. While pricing is often the subject of extensive negotiation and documentation, the general idea is that there is a pricing period that starts when the company "puts" the stock to the investors, and concludes some number of days thereafter (typically anywhere from five to ten trading days). The actual price is typically determined by picking, for example, the lowest volume weighted average price during the pricing period and paying some negotiated discount off that price.

Pros

- *Pricing.* While equity line pricing is not as favorable as ATMs, it can be less dilutive than other small-cap financing structures with discounts of 5 percent quite common.

- *Flexibility.* Since the company controls when it puts stock to investors, equity lines provide companies with flexibility.

- *Time/distraction.* Like ATMs, no roadshows are required, and limited management time is required.

- *Cost.* The cost of putting an equity line in place is similar to that of an ATM but is probably less than a follow-on.

  Cons

- *Financing size.* Equity lines are not well suited to companies that require material amounts of capital in one lump sum or in a short period of time.

- *Variable financing cost.* Because equity lines involve fixed pricing off of variable stock prices, the cost of capital fluctuates with the market. This can be good when the stock price is buoyant and less compelling when the stock price is depressed.

- *Time/registration risk.* Although a company with an effective registration statement can undertake an equity line quickly, a company contemplating an equity line that doesn't yet have an effective registration statement is subject to the vagaries of when the SEC may declare the registration statement effective once drafted and filed. Therefore, companies that need capital quickly shouldn't consider an equity line (except for WKSIs).

- *Optics/overhang.* Unlike an ATM where investors have no incentive to sell the company's stock short or to sell the stock they just purchased at market price, equity line investors typically make money by selling short the amount of stock that is put to them daily during the pricing period and then capturing the difference.[10] Therefore, the use of an equity line can put downward pressure on the stock price, provide disincentives for third parties to acquire the company's stock during periods where equity lines are being drawn upon, or, in the worst case, steer investors clear of the company's stock until the equity line is cancelled altogether.

TIP

In the past, many equity line investors had deservedly poor reputations. It wasn't uncommon for them to be offshore in order to, among other things, thwart detailed diligence, and the equity lines often employed were usurious. That is, unlike the lion's share of today's equity lines, equity line drawdowns were mandatory, not optional; floor prices were prohibited; and there were onerous fees for both commitment and termination. Equity lines became regarded as last gasp capital issued by shady investors to hapless companies. But subsequent to the financial crisis when growth capital was in dramatically short supply for small-cap companies, the equity line underwent somewhat of a renaissance; that is, many of the unsavory equity line investors exited the business because of redemption requests by their investors, and the new equity line investors became "the only game in town" for many small-cap companies. Accordingly, many of the equity lines available today are conspicuously more company friendly than they were in years past. For officers and directors considering an equity line structure, the **key point** is to focus on: (1) the ability of the company to, subject to certain conditions, access the equity line voluntarily and unilaterally; (2) pricing tied to volume weighted average pricing in lieu of closing bid prices; (3) the ability of the company to cancel the equity line at minimal expense whenever it wishes and undertake other forms of financing while the equity line is still in place; and (4) the ability of the company to set minimum prices to mitigate stock price erosion and dilution.

REGISTERED COMMON STOCK (REGISTERED DIRECT)

A registered direct ("RD") offering involves the sale of authorized, newly issued shares of registered common stock to accredited investors subsequent to a privately negotiated, confidential transaction. The primary difference between an RD and a restricted common stock structure is the timing of the registration of the stock. In a restricted common stock financing, the registration statement is filed after the deal is transacted; in an RD, the stock has been previously registered. An RD differs from a follow-on offering because it is a privately negotiated transaction that is announced only after it is consummated as opposed to a follow-on which is announced publicly first. Also, RDs aren't firmly underwritten as follow-ons are. Rather they are best efforts.

Pros

- *Stealth.* Because RDs are privately and confidentially negotiated, the company needn't telegraph its intentions to the marketplace subsequent to its registration statement being filed and declared effective.

- *Speed to market.* Once the company has an effective registration statement, it can undertake "shelf takedowns" quickly, sometimes in a matter of days from start to finish. Confidentiality in the RD process typically leads to more focused deal marketing, and obviates extended roadshows.

- *Pricing.* Because RDs involve the sale of registered stock, the discounts are typically smaller than if restricted common stock were sold (i.e., the investors don't have to absorb the impediment of pending registration). Moreover, RDs can often be priced more attractively than follow-on offerings because subsequent to the shelf being filed and declared effective, the deal is marketed privately (i.e., avoids the double discount phenomenon which sometimes occurs with follow-on offerings).

- *Simplicity.* From a balance sheet perspective as well as from a "Street" perspective, common stock is easily understood.

  Cons

- *Time/registration risk.* Although a company with an effective registration statement can undertake an RD quickly, a company contemplating an RD that doesn't yet have an effective registration statement is subject to the vagaries of when the SEC may declare the registration statement effective once drafted and filed. Therefore, companies that need capital quickly shouldn't consider a RD structure (except for WKSIs).

- *Offering size.* All the senior exchanges in the United States have rules that require shareholder approval prior to any privately negotiated offerings where the company seeks to sell a certain percentage (typically 20 percent) of the company's issued and outstanding stock at a discount to the closing bid price.

- *Shelf optics.* Even though the actual shelf takedown is confidentially transacted, filing a shelf in the first place is a conspicuously public event. Depending on the size of the shelf filed and the financial and operational strength of the company, the stock price can decrease in the immediate wake of a shelf filing, and the risk of this should be contemplated in the anticipated cost of capital analysis undertaken by officers and directors.[11]

REGISTERED COMMON STOCK (CONFIDENTIALLY MARKETED PUBLIC OFFERING)

A confidentially marketed public offering (CMPO) is very similar to an RD in that it involves the sale of authorized, newly issued shares of registered common stock to accredited investors subsequent to mostly confidential, private negotiations. The primary difference between a CMPO and an RD is that with a CMPO after the market closes on the night of pricing the offering, the company files a prospectus supplement and issues a press release to announce an overnight underwritten public offering. Accordingly, it's a hybrid RD and follow-on offering, which evolved principally to address the rules enacted by senior exchanges to stem the tide of privately negotiated, discounted transactions that sell material percentages (i.e., typically 20 percent or more) of companies without prior shareholder approval. Because the offering technically becomes a public offering when it is announced the night before being transacted, it circumvents the shareholder approval mechanism (i.e., it's no longer privately negotiated) and permits companies to sell more than 20 percent of the issued and outstanding shares without prior shareholder approval.

Pros

- *Stealth.* Because CMPOs are privately and confidentially negotiated, the company needn't telegraph its intentions to the marketplace subsequent to its registration statement being filed and declared effective. The stealth of a CMPO isn't affected by turning it into a public offering because notice is given after the market closes at night and before it opens the next morning.

- *Speed to market.* Once the company has an effective registration statement, it can undertake a CMPO quickly, sometimes in a matter of days from start to finish. Confidentiality in the CMPO process typically leads to more focused deal marketing and obviates extended roadshows.

- *Pricing.* Because CMPOs involve the sale of registered stock, the discounts are typically smaller than if restricted common stock were sold (i.e., the investors don't have to absorb the impediment of pending registration). Moreover, CMPOs can often be priced more attractively than follow-on offerings can be because subsequent to the shelf being filed and declared effective, the deal is marketed privately (i.e., avoids the double discount phenomenon that sometimes occurs with follow-on offerings).

- *Greater flexibility on offering size.* All the senior exchanges in the United States have rules which require shareholder approval prior to any privately negotiated offerings where the company seeks to sell a certain percentage (typically 20 percent) of the company's issued and outstanding stock at a discount to the closing bid price. Since CMPOs are publicly announced prior to being transacted, no such shareholder approval is required.

- *Underwritten.* CMPOs are fully underwritten, which means that once the investment banks present the terms of the financing to the company on the night of pricing and the terms are accepted, the company is very likely to get the funds.

- *Simplicity.* From a balance sheet perspective as well as from a "Street" perspective, common stock is easily understood.

  Cons

- *Time/registration risk.* Although a company with an effective registration statement can undertake a CMPO quickly, a company contemplating a CMPO that doesn't yet have an effective registration statement is subject to the vagaries of when the SEC may declare the registration statement effective once drafted and filed. Therefore, companies that need capital quickly shouldn't consider a CMPO structure (except for WKSIs).

- *Shelf optics.* Even though the actual shelf takedown is confidentially transacted, filing a shelf in the first place is a conspicuously public event. Depending on the size of the shelf filed and the financial and operational strength of the company, the stock price can decrease in the immediate wake of a shelf filing, and this risk should be contemplated in the anticipated cost of capital analysis undertaken by officers and directors.

TIP

Small-cap officers and directors often struggle with how to differentiate RDs, CMPOs, and follow-ons. This struggle is often exacerbated by (1) misunderstandings and biases of outspoken officers and directors and (2) investment bankers attempting to sway boards toward the structure that is most appealing and profitable to their bank. Since RDs and CMPOs are extremely similar (i.e., the only reason why a company would undertake a CMPO rather than an RD is if it would like to raise more than what exchange rules allow without a shareholder vote), the watershed decision from among the three is really whether to do a fully marketed follow-on or not. While there are, of course, no hard and fast rules in this regard, here are some key considerations for boards to analyze in order to remove some of the subjectivity and obfuscation.

First, the board should go to nasdaq.com, and print out the institutional holdings of four to six publicly traded industry peers and compare them. If the peer companies all have appreciably more institutional investors and more diverse institutional investors, then a follow-on could assist the company in enlarging and diversifying its institutional base to be more consistent with the peer group. Even a company that currently has 80 percent of its float owned by institutions still could benefit from a follow-on if it seeks to augment its shareholder base to include, for example, myriad mutual funds that are invested in the peer group, but not in the company. Second, if the company has never transacted a follow-on and the company became publicly listed through an alternative route (i.e. Form 10, reverse merger, etc.), then a follow-on could be considered a re-IPO—formally introducing the company to the "Street" in the same way an IPO roadshow does. Last, if the company has recently and conspicuously changed its business focus and its original institutional base has long since transitioned out of the stock, the board could also consider a follow-on. It perhaps goes without saying that the board needs to balance these three points against the time, management focus, and dilution. The **key point** here is that just because bulge bracket investment banks specialize in follow-ons doesn't mean that they're the right thing for every small-cap company. They might be, but they very well might not be. Last, there are often misconceptions that there is some minimum amount of capital that needs to be raised in order to transact a follow-on; this is simply not true. In 2011, for example, there were more than two dozen follow-ons that raised *less* than $50 million.

WARRANTS

Warrants aren't a financing structure per se. Rather they are financing sweeteners that are extremely common in small-cap finance. A warrant is in essence a call option— a right granted by the company to an investor to purchase a certain number of authorized, newly issued shares of restricted or registered common stock at a particular price for a negotiated period. Perhaps unlike any other element of small-cap corporate finance, warrants evoke a response—companies loathe them, and investors love them. Investors get them because they can. Companies issue them because they often have no choice.

- Investors like warrants for two principal reasons: (1) they are free[12] opportunities to positively augment their investment returns with little or no corresponding downside risk, and (2) depending upon a particular funds' accounting and valuation methodology, warrants can result in immediate gains to the funds' income statement.[13]

- Companies, on the other hand, detest issuing warrants because: (1) they can create an overhang on the stock that discourages new investors or makes subsequent fund raisings more challenging;

(2) they require expensive, recurring derivative accounting analysis; (3) they represent more prospective dilution; and (4) the derivative accounting charges negatively impact Generally Accepted Accounting Principles ("GAAP") results.

TIP

Even small-cap directors who are expert with respect to negotiating financings will often find themselves in situations where there is regrettably no bargaining leverage. As it pertains particularly to the issuance of warrants in connection with financings, the brutal reality is that warrants should be viewed by officers and directors as an incentive for the company to become stronger and larger, and in so doing move sufficiently along the bargaining continuum to be able to just say no. Until this happens, warrants are a way of life for many small-cap companies.

Even in the absence of too much negotiating leverage, companies can typically have some success in at least making sure that the amount of warrant coverage is consistent with what was issued in connection with recent peer financings. Although the negotiations can become onerous when it comes to some of the prototypical warrant features, there are at least four provisions that officers and directors should do their absolute best to resist:

1. *Penny warrants.* No matter how you slice it, penny warrants send a message of weakness to existing and future investors and can wreak havoc on capitalization tables. If the company has no choice but to issue them, the board should be vigilant about creative ways to retire them sooner as opposed to later. For example, the company can consider approaching new investors who would invest if there were no penny warrants and try to broker a deal that kills two birds with one stone.

2. *Full ratchet antidilution.* This common provision reduces the exercise price in a warrant to equal any subsequent financing at a lower price. Although the company may not be able to avoid issuing warrants with this downside price protection, officers and directors should at least try to negotiate that the full ratchet goes away after some period of time or becomes weighted average antidilution (less penal) after, perhaps, the achievement of some milestone. Officers and directors often infuriate investors by requesting that they waive the full ratchet postissuance which is what antidilution is intended to address. If such a waiver is sought, the company should be prepared to offer remuneration and be prepared to have the waiver request declined.

3. *Exploding warrants.* Even experienced officers, directors, and counsel can miss this type of antidilution protection in the definitive deal documents related to a financing. These provisions call for not only full-ratchet price protection but also more warrants to be issued to make the warrant holders whole after the impending dilution. These provisions are always laboriously worded on purpose; antidilution provisions in warrants should be read very carefully.

4. *Cashless exercise.* Although of little consequence with penny warrants, companies should strenuously argue for cash exercise (i.e., the investor is required to pay the company the product of the exercise price multiplied by the number of warrants being exercised) instead of net settlement in stock. If the company is going to issue a call option for free, it might as well receive the cash upon exercise.

THE OPTIMAL STRUCTURE

The structure of a financing is always important, but its impact on the company is directly proportional to the ratio of capital being raised to market capitalization. For example, if a $500 million company needs to raise $1 million, the difference between an optimal structure and a sub-optimal structure is negligible. However, since most financings in the small-cap realm involve companies selling material portions of their outstanding shares, the analysis by officers and directors of an optimal financing structure can have a significant impact. As is the case with other elements of governance, boards are best served by employing a methodical analysis of what type of financing structure best suits the company:[14]

1. *Balance sheet.* Analyzing what type of financing best fits a
    company's balance sheet is necessarily case specific, especially
    in the small-cap ecosystem where financial health can vary
    dramatically. Rather than getting mired down in balance sheet
    ratio minutiae, for fast-growing companies with no or minimal
    cash flow, equity is always preferential to debt. For slower-
    growth companies with more reliable cash flow, debt can be
    more advantageous especially when dilution is obviated. The
    conundrum that faces fast-growing small-cap companies is that
    they often have the weakest balance sheets to begin with, and
    thus wield less bargaining power to undertake financings that
    could optimize their balance sheets instead of denigrate them.
    Another key variable discussed earlier that impacts balance
    sheet analysis is time, which is often of the essence in small-cap
    financings so companies are often forced to transact whatever
    type of financing structure will bring them capital the fastest.
    The **key point** here is that analyzing the type of financing
    structure that is best for a small-cap company's balance sheet

can't be based simply on ratios from academic texts. Rather, board members must be realistic in determining what's optimal under the circumstances.

2. *Zeitgeist.* A mistake small-cap boards make repeatedly is pursuing and/or agreeing to a financing structure that fundamentally doesn't fit their company's individual needs, expectations, and trajectory. For example, companies far too often raise too little capital, more capital than they need (i.e., unnecessary dilution), or inexplicably risk the future of the company by putting the timing of a mission critical financing into the hands of the SEC's review of their registration statement. This shortsightedness happens most often in connection with structured financings like convertible notes. For example, agreeing to a balloon payment in year three without thoroughly thinking through whether that schedule actually matches the likely trajectory of the business, or commencing note repayment in stock after only six months when the company won't realistically achieve any milestones to drive investor interest for at least one year. The **key point** here is that just because a structure is good for the balance sheet and less dilutive than other alternatives still doesn't necessarily mean that it fits the company's overall needs and trajectory.

TIP

Failing to thoroughly think through what structure is the most optimal for the company's likeliest risks and challenges often leads to unnecessary dilution, wasted time, and higher transaction costs. But it often also results in something that is even more problematic for shareholders—renegotiating with investors. Small-cap directors often fail to see that from an institutional investor's viewpoint, renegotiating the terms of a financing (a "work-out") isn't

driven by conciliation but by profit. When boards seek to renegoti-
ate terms of a financing or seek waivers for particular provisions,
they erode confidence, pure and simple. And in order to compensate investors for greater perceived risk, a higher return is sought.
The **key point** here is that while no small-cap board can predict
the future with pinpoint precision, failing to adequately analyze
the fit of a structure in advance can cost shareholders dearly down
the road.

3. *Optics.* Because small-cap companies often require periodic
    infusions of growth capital, boards need to analyze how a
    particular financing structure will be perceived not only by
    shareholders and prospective open market investors, but also
    by those who could conceivably provide the next tranche of
    growth capital. For example, an existing shareholder might
    be nonplussed by a convertible note with full ratchet
    antidilution, but an otherwise interested institutional investor
    might walk away from providing growth capital to the
    company in a subsequent financing if the ratchet is triggered.
    The **key point** here is that in addition to assessing the likely
    impact on existing shareholders, boards of companies that
    will likely require subsequent financings need to be mindful of
    how a particular financing structure is going to impact future
    financing terms and viability. The most objective way for
    officers and directors to undertake this analysis is to find peer
    companies that recently employed the contemplated financing
    structure and review how the structure affected their stock
    price. Officers and directors should compare those findings to
    peer companies that employed different financing structures
    as well.[15]

THE MOST LIKELY STRUCTURE

More often than not, the practical ability for small-cap companies to undertake the financing structure that is optimal for their shareholders is based on a Darwinist continuum. On one end, there are the strongest, most actively traded companies with all the alternatives, and at the other end are the weakest, most sparsely traded companies with decidedly fewer choices. While small-cap companies occupy the full width of the continuum to be sure, the majority of them occupy the more challenging end to varying degrees. Though anathema to mid- and large-cap directors, it's an austere fact of life for those small-cap companies that the financing structure that might well be best for shareholders is often not even on the menu.

TIP

There are two things that most small-cap companies lack and definitely can't afford to waste—time and money. The way many small-cap companies (and some investment banks) go about preparing for a financing can waste conspicuous amounts of both. Perhaps more than anything else, small-cap directors need to be brutally realistic about the size, health, and capital markets profile of their company. Most people would view the chances of a slightly built, five-foot five-inch college senior pursuing a career as an NFL linebacker as about the same as many small-cap companies have of transacting a particular financing structure, yet there is often a collective disregard for the obvious. Why? Two principal reasons: (1) small-cap officers and directors are often considerably more *optimistic* than *realistic*; and (2) the ability for small-cap companies to transact a particular financing is driven largely by statistics that the vast majority of officers and directors don't know exist. The **key point** here is that small-cap officers and directors need to be students of financing data because the financing structure available for many small-cap companies will often be governed considerably more by recent peer financings than by what a board believes is optimal. Ignoring this doesn't change the financing outcome. It just wastes shareholder resources.

Simply put, determinations by a small-cap board regarding the optimal size, timing, and structure of a prospective financing *must* be juxtaposed with what is most likely. For example, consider the following 2011 deal data from PrivateRaise, which depict which financing structures were utilized most often out of the total number of financings in each market capitalization segments:

Companies with $100 Million Market Capitalization or Less*

Restricted common stock	44%
Equity line	13%
Convertible debt	12%
Convertible preferred	11%
RD	10%
CMPO	4%
ATM	3%
Follow-on	3%

*Note that 56 percent of these financings had warrants and that median warrant coverage was 50 percent.

Companies with $100–$250 Million Market Capitalization*

Restricted common stock	35%
CMPO	14%
ATM	11%
Convertible preferred	10%
RD	10%
Convertible debt	7%
Follow-on	7%
Equity line	6%

*Note that 33 percent of these financings had warrants and that median warrant coverage was 50 percent.

Companies with $250–$500 Million Market Capitalization*

Restricted common stock	28%
Follow-on	24%
CMPO	18%
RD	8%
ATM	6%
Equity line	6%
Convertible preferred	5%
Convertible debt	5%

*Note that 22 percent of these financings had warrants and that median warrant coverage was 50 percent.

Companies with $500 Million–$1 Billion Market Capitalization*

Restricted common stock	25%
ATM	23%
CMPO	18%
Follow-on	15%
Convertible preferred	8%
Convertible debt	8%
RD	3%
Equity line	—

*Note that 6 percent of these financings had warrants and that median warrant coverage was 75 percent.

Companies with $1 Billion–$5 Billion Market Capitalization*

ATM	39%
Follow-on	29%
Restricted common stock	20%
CMPO	4%
Convertible preferred	4%
Convertible debt	3%
RD	1%
Equity line	—

*Note that 4 percent of these financings had warrants and that median warrant coverage was 33 percent.

There are some compelling takeaways from these data:

- The combination of ATMs, RDs, CMPOs, and follow-ons (typically the least dilutive of the eight common structures) comprised only

20 percent of the financings for companies with less than $100 million in market capitalization, while they comprised 73 percent of the financings for companies with between $1 billion and $5 billion in market capitalization. Just making the jump to companies with market capitalizations of $100 million to $250 million more than doubled the percentage of ATMs, RDs, CMPOs, and follow-ons to 42 percent. In other words, the larger the company, the more opportunities there are to do less dilutive financings.

- The data show that the opposite is also true. For companies under $100 million in market capitalization 67 percent of the financings were restricted common stock and convertible instruments (typically the most dilutive), while that percentage dropped almost 60 percent for companies with market capitalizations of between $1 billion and $5 billion.

- Equity lines comprise nearly 20 percent of all financings for companies below $250 million in market capitalization but only 6 percent of all financings for companies between $250 million and $5 billion in market capitalization.

- ATMs appear to have little correlation to market capitalization, inasmuch as on a transaction count basis (instead of percentage), there were 23 ATMs put in place for companies below $100 million in market capitalization, and there were 29 put in place for companies with market capitalizations of between $1 billion and $5 billion.

- Predictably, CMPOs have an inverse relationship to market capitalization inasmuch as the structure is principally designed to raise more capital than would otherwise be permitted by so-called "20 percent" rules. On a transaction count basis, there were 26 CMPOs transacted by companies with less than $100 million in market capitalization, while there were only 3 for companies with market capitalizations of between $1 billion and $5 billion.

- There is a clear inverse correlation between the percentage of financings containing warrants and issuer market capitalization.

The irony of these highly instructive data is that institutional investors and investment bankers review them all the time, yet the one group that arguably should make use of these data more than anyone else—small-cap officers and directors—virtually *never* do. And these data are only the proverbial tip of the iceberg because they can be honed down to the peer level to provide information that is even more granular and telling.[16] How can the board of a $150 million company, for example, conceivably make an informed determination about the type of financing structure to pursue without first appreciating that there is a 75 percent likelihood that it will undertake a restricted common stock, convertible, or equity line financing (and a four in ten chance that it will issue 50 percent warrant coverage)? It's hard to know what's more poignant—how valuable these data are to boards or how rarely they are ever utilized.

Consider another example. The board of a $300 million market capitalization company (with stock that trades about $350,000 per day) decides that its optimal financing structure is a registered common stock offering in order to raise $50 million. In the absence of any data, the board begins to make the necessary preparations with counsel to draft its Form S-3 registration statement. If the board actually reviewed relevant data it would likely be heartened to learn that 50 percent of the financings undertaken last year by companies its size were, indeed, RDs, CMPOs, and follow-ons. On the other hand, though, if it reviewed the data set forth below, it wouldn't be terribly pleased to learn that for a company its size, the median trading volume for companies transacting RDs, CMPOs, and follow-ons was almost twice its amount ($680,000 per day) and that the median deal size was equivalent to 40 days of trading (which in this case would be only $14 million instead of the $50 million sought by the board):

All RDs, CMPOs, and Follow-ons for the Period 2010–2012 (by Market Capitalization)[17]

$50 million–$150 million: median trading volume $275,000 per day, median deal equaled 42 days of trading

$150 million–$300 million: median trading volume $680,000 per day, median deal equaled 40 days of trading

$300 million–$500 million: median trading volume $1.8 million per day, median deal equaled 33 days of trading

$500 million–$1 billion: median trading volume $4.1 million per day, median deal equaled 24 days of trading

Of course, a company's use of statistics like these isn't intended to be determinative, but rather advisory. That is, officers and directors need to be principally guided by what's best for shareholders and not just by what is most likely or unlikely; and for every statistic there is an exception. The **key point** here is that given the uniqueness of the small-cap ecosystem, boards risk doing a material disservice to shareholders by reaching conclusions about how much money to raise, when, and with what structure without carefully factoring in what's most likely. Conversely, boards that undertake a careful preliminary analysis of what type of financing is possible, preferable, and likely are in the best position to hire an investment bank that is suited to the task at hand.

Notes

1. The order is based on 2011 statistics from PrivateRaise, Dealogic, and Capital IQ. The structures set forth in this chapter are those that are most common. Commercial credit facilities and, factoring, for example, are also common in small-cap companies, but since those financing vehicles are widely understood and not unique to small-cap companies, this book doesn't include any additional commentary about them. Other financings (e.g., strategic investments, 144a offerings, etc.) certainly occur in the small-cap realm but with a fraction of the frequency of those set forth here.

2. Directors should work with management and counsel to make sure that they understand how the recently amended Rule 144 provisions apply to their company.

3. When investors effectuate a short sale, they borrow stock, sell it in the market, and hope the stock declines in value so that when they deliver the shares back, they pay less for them than what they were worth when they borrowed them, thereby resulting in a gain.

4. The reason why convertible pricing is typically less discounted than restricted common stock is twofold: (1) even though the common stock underlying the convertible instrument is restricted at issuance, investors are offered compensation to wait for registration and profitable conversion in the form of a dividend and liquidation priority; and (2) many institutional investors account for convertible instruments at par so that their investment returns are less affected by price volatility in the underlying common stock.

5. The common stock underlying convertible preferred instruments can sometimes be registered at issuance or unregistered at issuance; it's subject to negotiation. If the underlying common stock is unregistered at issuance, then the same "registration restrictions and penalties" caveat from restricted common stock offerings applies as well.

6. The common stock underlying convertible note instruments can sometimes be registered at issuance or unregistered at issuance; it's subject to negotiation. If the underlying common stock is unregistered at issuance, then the same "registration restrictions and penalties" caveat from restricted common stock offerings applies.

7. Occasionally, companies also sell preferred stock as well as American depository receipts (ADR) in ATMs.

8. Secondary shares (i.e., insider shares) can also be sold through ATMs.

9. There is one principal exception to this admonishment: well-known seasoned issuers (WKSIs). Simply put, a WKSI is a company that has or recently had a market capitalization of $700 million (based on issued and outstanding shares held by non-affiliates) or in the last three years issued at least $1 billion aggregate number of primary, nonconvertible securities for cash. Companies that are WKSIs can file Form S-3 registration statements that are essentially deemed effective upon filing.

10. Officers and directors often fail to understand why equity lines are attractive to investors. Though highly simplified for purposes of illustration, consider the following. A company puts 10 shares of stock to the investor, which the investor is contractually bound to purchase after a week-long pricing period. In accordance with the equity line contract, the investor is, for example, guaranteed to pay 95 percent of the lowest volume weighted average closing price during that week for all 10 shares. If the investor sells 2 shares each day during the pricing period for 5 days at the volume weighted average price of that day, the investor is going to make a minimum of 5 percent (gross of costs, expenses, taxes, etc.) on the day when the stock is at the lowest volume weighted average price, and more than 5 percent on the days when the stock has a higher volume weighted average price.

11. Although it varies depending upon the market capitalization of the company and the size of the shelf (among other things), it's not uncommon for companies that file shelf registration statements to experience up to a 5 percent decrease in stock price

in the ensuing 30 trading days. Depending upon individual company circumstances, it's not uncommon to see that initial decrease eventually normalize.

12. There are occasions when investors pay for warrants, but quite often they are simply issued in small-cap financings as sweeteners—for free. When it comes to exercising warrants, some require holders to pay cash for the exercise price, and some warrants permit cashless exercise.

13. Small-cap officers and directors often don't completely appreciate fund management accounting drivers which can make warrants attractive to hedge funds. There are some hedge funds that ascribe no value whatsoever to warrants unless or until the warrants are exercised, or the actual warrants are sold to a third party. Hedge funds that do value warrants when issued tend to mark them at some predetermined percentage of the Black-Scholes value; the three main inputs to determine Black-Scholes valuation are time (the amount of time remaining for the warrant), intrinsic value (market price for the stock less the strike price of the warrant), and volatility. Given the high volatility quotient for many small-cap stocks and the five- to seven-year duration of many warrants, even if the warrants lack intrinsic value, they can still add incremental profit depending upon how aggressively or conservatively a given fund accounts for them. There are some hedge funds that value warrants at their full Black-Scholes valuation upon receipt, regardless of whether they can be exercised or not. Reasonable people will differ on the propriety of this, but it's important, nevertheless, for officers and directors to understand what's driving the motivations of funds that seek material warrant coverage. It's especially important to be mindful of these fund accounting treatments when companies attempt to offer, for example, inducements so that investors will exercise their warrants. Officers and directors often can't understand why investors wouldn't want to exercise in-the-money warrants (even if the strike price is lowered as an inducement), whereas hedge funds actually might be taking a hit to their profit because they are going to lose the volatility and time values when the warrants are exercised.

14. There are myriad small-cap companies that are not in a position to negotiate prospective financings to any appreciable degree because they're operationally and financially challenged to such an extent that they simply require an infusion of growth capital to live for another day. Even in dire circumstances boards should exercise care to avoid entering into financing structures that are a conspicuously poor fit for the company.

15. Wherever possible, companies should not outsource this analysis to the company's investment bankers because of the inherent conflict of interest. The analysis should be done in-house or by an independent third party.

16. As mentioned earlier, these data are available to the public from PrivateRaise, Dealogic, Knobias, PlacementTracker, and Capital IQ (or a combination of all five).

17. These statistics were compiled by Roth Capital Partners based on data from Dealogic and Capital IQ.

CHAPTER 3

HIRING THE RIGHT INVESTMENT BANK— EVERY TIME

Hiring the Right Investment Bank

Key considerations for directors:

- Small-cap companies can't effectively shop for the right investment bank if they don't know what they're buying first.
- Though rarely utilized, data should drive investment banking selection—not the data supplied by investment banks in their marketing materials.
- There are special considerations companies should take into account when they retain investment banks for ATMs, RDs, CMPOs, and follow-ons.

Common mistakes to avoid:

- Small-cap companies are often too quick to default to the company's existing bankers for a prospective financing—they might be the best choice, but they might not be.
- Officers and directors tend to inexplicably avoid the most valuable due-diligence step when retaining an investment bank—speaking to former bank clients.
- Just because a large investment bank shows interest in working with a small-cap company doesn't mean that bank is a good choice.

I magine for a moment that you are arriving in a foreign country's airport and need to exchange U.S. dollars for the local currency. The principal method for changing currency in the airport is to hand dollars to the kiosk teller and in return receive local currency based on a good-faith estimate of the value of the two currencies. Several yards past the exchange kiosk, the tourists are asked, "Do you think you are proficient in exchanging dollars for the local currency?" The vast majority responds in the affirmative. As proof they point to the foreign currency in their wallets and also mention that the kiosk teller confirmed that they were getting a great exchange rate. Few of the tourists are aware, or wait around long enough for the pollster to inform them, that there actually is an official daily exchange rate and that they didn't have to use the honor system at all.

In a nutshell, this is the conundrum of discussing investment banking with many small-cap companies. Too often, officers and directors feel as if they need no assistance in hiring investment banks because they've done so in the past and not only raised capital but also received assurances from their bankers that the terms were the best available in the market. But just as the travelers were confident of their currency acumen until they learned that there was an actual exchange rate that obviated the honor system, small-cap officers and directors need to swap the honor system for a more objective capital raising methodology. Developing a more quantitative way to select investment bankers is a critical component of this.

THE IMPORTANCE OF THE TIMELINE

The analyses discussed in Chapters 1 and 2 precede this chapter for a simple, albeit often disregarded, reason: given the *dramatically disparate nature of small-cap financings* and the *heightened potential for conflicts of interest* in small-cap investment banking, companies can't reliably select the best-suited investment bank without first having an advanced understanding of what type of financing is both possible and likely.

More specifically, small-cap financings range from nine-digit follow-on offerings for companies that trade dozens of millions of dollars of stock per day to six-digit, privately negotiated, highly structured convertible instruments for nascent companies that trade less than $50,000 of stock per day—and everything in between. Not only are there no investment banks that specialize in the entire continuum, but there are some banks that are so specialized that they might, for example, transact only four or five restricted common stock financings per year exclusively for mining companies. Therefore, small-cap companies might not fail, but they will absolutely underperform by shopping for investment banks before they know what they are buying.

With respect to potential conflicts of interest, it's important to be clear. Small-cap investment banks, by and large, are not paid ongoing retainers for providing financing advice. They are paid a negotiated percentage of the gross amount of a consummated financing. In short, small-cap bankers typically don't get paid unless boards agree to transact the banker-recommended financing. Without passing any explicit or implicit judgments in this regard, bankers with this fee arrangement have a potential conflict of interest. That is, the financing recommendation can be jaded by the bank's interest in getting paid. While the vast majority of small-cap investment bankers are knowledgeable, dedicated, and passionate about financing growth companies, like any profession there are also charlatans. Therefore, directors have no choice on behalf of shareholders but to at the least be cognizant of the potential conflict of interest. The most expedient way for small-cap officers and directors to maximize shareholder value and simultaneously mitigate potential conflicts of interest in connection with financings is to be informed consumers of investment banking services.

DATA ARE THE STARTING POINT

Having determined their gating issues, the amount of capital sought, the use of proceeds, and the preferable and most likely financing structure, companies need to refine that information into a focused set of questions in order to hone in on the investment bank best suited to the company's needs.

For example, Company A is a medical device company with a $100 million market capitalization that trades $100,000 per day. Company A would like to raise $5 million–$7 million of growth capital, and from data the officers and directors have reviewed, they believe that the best and likeliest financing structure for the company is either a restricted common stock offering or a convertible preferred instrument.

Because the process of successfully transacting a private placement like this for a company this size is a radically different proposition from transacting a registered offering, for example, for a company four times the size, finding the best-suited investment bank to help Company A is predominantly an exercise in finding investment banks that have *recent experience* doing what the company needs done.[1]

Recent experience is critical for two reasons: (1) the universe of investors that invest capital directly into small-cap companies is quite fluid. Therefore, an investment bank's investor contacts from two years ago might not be helpful now; and (2) depending upon what's happening in the broader stock market, various different kinds of financing structures and terms can go in and out of style. So Company A should be looking for banks that have direct experience in the last 12 months (6 months is even better).

Experience doing the same or a substantially similar type of financing is critical because time is often of the essence in small-cap financings. While many banks might conceivably be able to help find financing for Company A, banks that recently transacted the same or substantially similar financings arguably have the best chance of delivering timely results. In a world in which nearly every investment bank professes to be "number one" at something and touts the number of financings it has transacted, for small-cap companies, what's really most instructive is considerably more refined—when is the last time the investment bank transacted exactly what the company needs?

TIP

Relationships between companies and investment banks, like any professional services relationships, can become understandably close over time because of common experiences and even friendships. Far too many small-cap boards make the mistake of defaulting to the investment bank that did its last financing (or all its previous financings) for the next financing either because of loyalty or expedience. To be clear, the investment bank previously used by the company could well be a good choice, especially since the bank knows the company and its business better than a newcomer would. But, it also could be a terrible choice, and the "default" status suggests that the company will never find out. As suggested earlier, it is rare that a small-cap investment bank will have equal experience and proficiency with small restricted stock offerings, ATMs, and follow-ons. The **key point** here is that given how fluid and disparate the small-cap fundraising marketplace is, small-cap officers and directors would be wise to view each successive financing as a discrete event for which new banking mandates need to be earned. As a result, there is a better chance that officers and directors will objectively select the best investment bank to assist the company, instead of simply defaulting to the one they know. If the company's existing or frequent banker is found to be the one best suited for the prospective financing after taking into account the totality of the circumstances, that is, of course, fine.

Company A needs to look first for investment banks that in the last six months to a year have transacted private placements of restricted stock for medical device companies with the same or substantially similar capital markets profiles (e.g., market capitalization, trading volume, and exchange). If there are none, then Company A can broaden the search to include private placements of restricted stock for nonmedical device companies with the same or substantially similar capital markets profiles as Company A. If that search also bears no fruit, then the search can be broadened to simply include investment banks that have transacted private placements of restricted stock in similar dollar increments (i.e. $5 million to $7 million). Again, the purpose here is simply to quantitatively screen for investment banks using available data[2] that have the most *recent* (preceding 6 to 12 months), *relevant* (structure, financing size, industry, market capitalization, trading volume, and exchange) experience.

REFINING THE RESULTS

Once investment banks with the most recent, relevant experience are identified, the next step is to determine which of the banks is the best value for the money. Companies can listen to representatives from each bank explain why their bank offers the best value proposition, but officers and directors invariably need to "trust but verify."

There are several ways for companies to do this that are neither costly nor particularly time consuming. It's hard to know what's more surprising in this regard—how rarely companies actually make the effort or how instructive the results are:

1. *Check references.* For some reason, officers and directors are highly reluctant to take the most informative step in determining whether a particular investment bank is best suited for their company—speaking to the most recent peer clients.[3] The purpose of speaking to former clients is threefold:

(a) to find out whether the investment bank conducted thorough due diligence on the prior clients (i.e., failure to conduct thorough due diligence is often a harbinger of poor attention to detail and an inability to attract appropriate investors); (b) to discern whether the investment bank has a pattern of overpromising and underdelivering; and (c) to compile any anecdotal comments that may warrant further inquiry. What could be more helpful than speaking to former clients, especially considering that it's free, and officers and directors are usually happy to provide information?

2. *Pricing.* In addition to what is gleaned from speaking to former clients, companies need to take an added step in order to quantify the results of the bank's most recent transactions. For example, if there were four common stock financings in the last six months for medical device companies with substantially similar capital markets profiles to Company A, how did the investment bank's results for similar financings compare? While there are sometimes good reasons why terms can be variable from one small-cap company to the next, a pattern of financings by a particular investment bank that are more dilutive than the average clearly should be closely investigated.

3. *Trading.* The company also needs to examine what happened in the 30 to 60 days subsequent to the public announcements of recent, similar financings. Did the stock of those issuers plummet, stay relatively flat, or go up? Again, to be clear, there are many things that induce movement in small-cap stocks, and it's unfair to hold investment bankers responsible for them all. However, a pattern of postdeal share price drawdowns in successive financings is definitely something worth further inquiry.

4. *Fee.* Last, but certainly not least, finding the best value for
    money requires a fee comparison. While this is certainly
    something that rarely escapes the attention of officers and
    directors, banking fees are highly disparate in the small-cap
    ecosystem and can't be compared in a vacuum. Moreover,
    it's not uncommon for smaller companies to pay investment
    banking fees partly with cash and partly with warrants. If that's
    being considered, the company should make sure it asks former
    banking clients how the bank comported itself with respect to
    monetizing warrants.

TIP

As is often the case with hiring different kinds of professional
service providers, companies can understandably be induced to hire
investment banks because of a particularly skilled, experienced,
charismatic banker. And similar to law, PR, advertising, audit, and
so on, the firm being hired is only as good as the main person who
is servicing the company's account. As it pertains to banking, the
key point here is that if the company is primarily retaining an investment bank because of an individual or two, the officers and directors
would be well served to take the additional step of confirming with
former clients that those individuals actually played material roles
in their financings.

SPECIAL CONSIDERATIONS FOR SELECTING ATM BANKERS

As discussed in Chapter 2, ATMs are unique financing mechanisms
because of the sale of stock intraday into the natural flow of trading and
the ability for issuers to control the timing, size, volume, and price of

each ATM sale. Consequently, there are some additional issues companies should consider when evaluating prospective ATM banks:

1. *Process.* Given the high degree of interaction between issuer and banker with ATM sales, it's critical that the process and communication be seamless. Therefore, it's equally critical to ensure that previous clients confirm that seamless communication.

2. *Conflicts.* Unique conflicts of interest can arise in ATM settings which are easy to overlook. For example, investment banks that either make a market in the company's stock or engage in proprietary trading that might include the company's stock can create an incentive for those banks to elevate the profitable execution of bank trades over the company's ATM sales. Companies should exercise care to qualify those risks prior to engaging any ATM bank.

3. *ATM unavailability.* Because ATMs involve intraday sales of registered stock into the flow of trading at the direction of the company, there are certain situations in which banks make the ATMs unavailable; for example, material news pending and insufficient trading volume. Some ATM bankers are more restrictive than others in this regard, and some are less clear than others about the matter. Therefore, companies need to make sure that the restrictions are clear and that prior clients confirm that the restrictions were reliably and predictably enforced.

4. *Trading.* One of the primary benefits of ATMs is that undiscounted shares are sold directly into the flow of trading. But ATM sales can be transacted with minimal impact, or they can be more clumsily executed. Therefore, it's important for companies that are comparing different prospective ATM

bankers to review: (a) the median postfiling change in stock price after one day; and (b) how the client's stocks performed during ATM sales periods compared to relevant benchmarks (e.g., Nasdaq Biotech Index, Nasdaq Small-cap Tech, etc.). The reason why the median stock performance the day after filing the ATM is important is that institutional investors are often astute students of ATM banking acumen, and over time the median change in stock price of multiple companies can depict a telling pattern of market confidence or lack thereof in a particular ATM bank's performance. Moreover, since ATM sales are intended to be transacted into the natural flow of trading, the median performance of ATM client's stock over time should be in concert with benchmarked peers; a pattern of median underperformance should be investigated further.

SPECIAL CONSIDERATIONS FOR SELECTING RD AND CMPO BANKERS

RDs and CMPOs are very similar financing transactions in that they both predominantly involve privately negotiated sales of registered common stock. Like ATMs, hiring bankers to undertake RDs or CMPOs requires some special consideration by small-cap officers and directors:

1. *Pricing.* There are two salient metrics that boards should consider reviewing when comparing investment banks in connection with RDs and CMPOs: (a) the median change in stock price from filing date to pricing; and (b) the median change in stock price between the deal announcement and five trading days thereafter. As discussed in Chapter 2, the very act of filing a Form S-3 registration statement can precipitate selling of a company's stock because the shelf filing signals impending dilution. The goal of every company when transacting a RD or CMPO is for the lowering in stock price,

if any, to be as small as practicable from when the shelf is filed to when a transaction is priced. Some banks are better than others at executing RDs and CMPOs with less dilution, and companies should be cognizant of this when selecting a bank. Moreover, it's also important to consider the median stock performance five trading days after a RD or CMPO is announced because investment banks that serially inject short-term holders into their financings will have poor results during this period as the faster money seeks to exit their positions.

TIP

There are investment banks that are reluctant to openly collaborate with companies with respect to which investors will be included in RDs and CMPOs (and follow-ons), and how many shares will be allocated to each of them (the process is often referred to as "book building" or "allocations") in the financing. Officers and directors should confirm in advance what the investment bank's policy is in this regard and confirm with prior clients that the policy was, in fact, followed. An open, collaborative allocation process is crucial for two reasons that small-cap companies routinely overlook: (a) if the purpose of the RD or CMPO is to expand the shareholder base to include certain funds, or certain kinds of funds, board pricing committees need to be able to verify during the allocation process that those goals are being achieved; and (b) whether investment banks admit it or not, there is a temptation for banks to offer shares to good clients regardless of whether those investors are suitable and appropriate for a given financing or not, and companies can't effectively mitigate that risk without open access. It's worth noting that even when allocation information is openly shared, small-cap boards are often still at a practical disadvantage (without capital markets or corporate finance experts on many boards, directors often have no realistic ability to know whether the allocations being recommended are appropriate or not). Accordingly, the **key point** here is that if the board lacks this acumen, it should consider retaining an independent third-party expert (whose compensation is not linked to the consummation of the transaction) to advise the board on whether the allocations being recommended are consistent with the board's objectives.

2. *Market making.* One of the biggest capital markets challenges for many small-cap companies is that too few broker-dealers make a market in their stocks. (This subject is discussed in greater detail in Part Two.) Companies that suffer from having a stock that is materially less liquid than stocks of their peers should confirm that the investment banks under consideration for transacting a RD or CMPO actively make markets in their clients' stocks after a financing, if they don't already. The easiest way to confirm this is to speak to prior banking clients.

3. *Banker's counsel.* Unless officers and directors have participated in numerous RDs or CMPOs, they are unlikely to have experienced how impactful an investment bank's counsel can be on the financing process (and not in a positive way). Simply put, investment banks occasionally choose attorneys who, while from large well-known law firms, have demonstrably little experience with small-cap financings like RDs and CMPOs and consequently can cause material delays that in the worst-case scenario can actually jeopardize financings. Therefore, the company should proactively ask which counsel each investment bank under consideration intends to use and ask former clients about their experience in working with those attorneys.

4. *Special CMPO issues.* As discussed previously, RDs and CMPOs are substantially similar, but CMPOs involve the added step of flipping the transaction to a public offering the night before

pricing. If the company is planning to undertake a CMPO, there are two additional issues to consider when choosing an investment bank: (a) companies should confirm with prior clients that the CMPO process was handled seamlessly by the investment banks under consideration (i.e., assistance with necessary filings, any additional underwriting processes, public announcement, interactions with regulatory agencies and exchanges, etc.); and (b) companies should consider limiting the investment banks under consideration to only those with material CMPO experience. This last point is particularly important, because investment banks that don't have material experience with CMPOs are not only more likely to experience problems with the CMPO process, but they are also more likely to try to persuade boards to undertake follow-ons instead.

SPECIAL CONSIDERATIONS FOR SELECTING FOLLOW-ON BANKS[4]

The banking process for follow-ons is materially different from other small-cap financings. There are some unique considerations for officers and directors to weigh in selecting the right investment banks for follow-ons.

1. *Bookrunners.* Choosing bookrunners for a follow-on often creates anxiety among small-cap officers and directors because of fundamental misunderstandings about the bookrunner's role and value to the company:

    a. *Selection:* Simply put, selecting bookrunners often comes down to the connection between two critical issues for small-cap companies—which investment bank has the best historic bookrunning performance metrics[5] *and* which bank has the equity research analyst who the company believes can be (or has been) most influential for the company's capital markets objectives. More specifically, the historic bookrunning performance metrics to consider, among others, are the median change in stock price between the filing dates and the pricing dates,[6] and the median change in stock price between the pricing dates and 45 days thereafter.[7] As it pertains to equity analysts, companies typically ascertain which equity analysts are the most highly regarded by discourse with existing and targeted investors. If the most sought after analyst is already covering the company, then the company might well consider giving that factor greater weight in the bookrunner selection process. If the influential analysts don't currently write research on the company, then the company needs to gauge whether the sought after equity analysts are sufficiently inclined toward the company and factor that into the selection process.[8]

TIP

When selecting bookrunners, in particular the lead left bookrunner, small-cap companies are often unduly influenced by the stature of banks. Choosing a "name brand" or "bulge bracket" investment bank can, of course, be a good choice for the shareholders if the selection criteria set forth above dictate the same. However, officers and directors need to be vigilant to make sure when choosing a large investment bank as a lead left bookrunner that: (a) recent peer clients were happy with the service; and (b) there aren't very large (i.e., more profitable) financings on the bank's deal calendar around the same time the company's financing is scheduled to price. The **key point** here is that large investment banks have large overhead expenses, and financings which aren't large enough to generate material profit are more likely to get less compelling resources and support. Also, it's important to be mindful that even if a bulge-bracket research analyst is positively predisposed to the company, institutional salespeople at large investment banks often have a very limited audience for diminutive small-cap companies (i.e., most clients could well be foreclosed by mandate from even considering stocks that are beneath a certain market capitalization). The **key point** here is that it's rarely a good thing to be the smallest company under coverage by an equity analyst at a large investment bank, especially for small-cap companies.

    b. *Logistics.* there aren't any hard and fast rules regarding how many bookrunners are optimal; for practical purposes, the fewer the better.[9] A **key point** that shouldn't be overlooked is that prior to selecting bookrunners, the company should confirm that the prospective lineup of investment banks[10] has recently worked together (in the anticipated roles) and that prior clients can confirm that the banks worked well together.

TIP

Companies shouldn't underestimate the wasteful shenanigans that can transpire among bookrunners. Notwithstanding the integrity and professionalism one would rightfully expect, bookrunners who don't work well together can get mired in name calling and half-truths calculated to preserve bragging rights and brand superiority. In fairness to investment banks, it is a high-stakes game where lead left assignments garner considerably more fees and a greater likelihood of additional lead left assignments. Because the toll of dysfunctional bookrunner situations can be material, small-cap officers and directors should think twice before selecting bookrunners who haven't worked together before.

    c. *Fees.* Bookrunner fees are investment banking's holy grail, and fee negotiations can be predictably contentious not just for the obvious reasons, but also because they can have precedential value when disclosed in the prospectus supplement. It perhaps goes without saying that the more bookrunners, the more challenging it can be to reach agreements on fees. Officers and directors who undertake these negotiations for the first time express exasperation because of, among other things, the dramatic posturing and seemingly endless haggling. There are two good rules of thumb for dealing with this problem: (i) review recent previous prospectus supplements to determine the fees that banks are receiving; and (ii) as is the case with many fee negotiations, plan on none of the parties being happy when the negotiations conclude.

2. *Comanagers.* There is often obfuscation about the role of comanagers and the reasons for selecting one rather than another. Bookrunners are chosen over comanagers because comanagers lack recent, relevant, compelling bookrunning experience or a highly influential equity analyst or both. Comanagers, in turn, are selected because they have influential equity analysts or because the comanaging firm has been particularly helpful to the company (i.e., time served) or both. Occasionally, and particularly in the small-cap ecosystem, particular comanagers might be sought because they have expertise in a valuable niche geography or have particular strength with sought after retail investors.

Ultimately, selecting an investment bank is an exercise that myriad small-cap officers and directors simply need to rethink. Unprepared, deferential outsourcing needs to be replaced with diligent, data-driven focus in order to mitigate unnecessary dilution, wasted time, and misspent money. Also, prior to dismissing the airport currency exchange hypothetical, board members should spend some time in the next board meeting frankly discussing the hypothetical's applicability to the company's prior financings—the conversation might result in some unexpectedly poignant conclusions.

Notes

1. It's worth noting that there are certainly circumstances in the small-cap ecosystem where it can and does make sense for companies to raise growth capital without the assistance of an investment bank, broker-dealer, finder, and so on; for example, they can negotiate directly with investors. If the company is doing the same or substantially similar financing it did previously with the same investors, a banker might be superfluous. Or there are circumstances where investors approach companies directly with terms that are sufficiently straightforward that an intermediary might not add material value. Last, there could be situations that are sufficiently dire that companies simply can't afford the time to get intermediaries involved. In all these circumstances small-cap directors need to make sure that management and counsel are confident that such financings don't run afoul of any state or federal securities laws and regulations or exchange rules (especially if the financing involves registered stock or insider participation).

2. The data referenced are in proprietary databases (fee accessible) owned by companies like PrivateRaise, Dealogic, Knobias, PlacementTracker or Capital IQ.

3. Previous publicly traded clients of investment banks are typically public information. So there are no protocols that require a prospective banking client to get prior oral or written permission in this regard.

4. Though not reiterated here, the same admonishment about collaborative allocation applies to follow-ons as much as to RDs and CMPOs.

5. For an investment bank to be considered for the "lead left" bookrunner position, the performance metrics should be limited to the occasions when the lead left candidate actually operated in that capacity. Considering a lead left candidate that has little or no lead left experience is a risk that companies should carefully consider taking.

6. Analyzing the investment bank's historic median filing to pricing statistics, as with RDs and CMPOs, gives officers and directors an objective indicator of the likely dilution they can expect. In this regard, less is certainly more.

7. Analyzing the investment bank's historic median pricing to 45 days out statistics measures something that is exclusive to follow-ons. Bookrunners often are granted an overallotment (or "green shoe") option for 30 days after the follow-on, which is, in effect, a federally sanctioned methodology for bookrunners to stabilize the price of the stock postoffering. Analyzing the period from pricing to 45 days out

enables boards to not only gauge the efficacy of price stabilization, but also what happens after the overallotment period concludes (i.e., if the deal was allocated, priced, and stabilized well, then there shouldn't be an appreciable median decrease in stock price during that entire period).

8. To be clear, equity research and investment banking are independent functions at investment banks and are often functionally and literally partitioned. Therefore, selecting an investment bank to underwrite a follow-on doesn't guarantee that an investment bank's equity research analyst will cover a new banking client or cover the client favorably. So companies need to become expert at the art and science of gauging whether research analysts are positively or negatively inclined toward them.

9. As discussed in Chapter 2, typically small-cap follow-ons have between two and three bookrunners.

10. More specifically, it's not only the banks that are important, but the actual bankers.

CHAPTER 4

THE UNLIKELY ROLE OF THE SMALL-CAP BOARD IN INVESTOR MEETINGS AND ROADSHOWS

The Importance of Investor Meetings

Key considerations for directors:

- Preparing for and conducting investor meetings have heightened importance for small-cap companies.
- Small-cap boards should determine what level of involvement they will have in the preparatory process.
- At a minimum, boards should consider reviewing the investor presentation materials with management prior to the actual meetings.
- The less experienced officers are with respect to corporate finance/capital markets, the more board oversight might be required.

Common mistakes to avoid:

- Small-cap directors can often be too deferential to management and banks with respect to preparing for and conducting investor meetings, especially considering the associated enterprise risks.
- Boards should be realistic about what investment banks are (and are not) going to do with respect to investor meetings.
- Boards should distinguish between investors and financiers.

S mall-cap directors need to be proactively involved in myriad issues that would never receive any attention from large-cap directors because potentially business-ending risks are everywhere in most small-cap companies. The "immune-suppressed" nature of small-cap companies leads to the need for board involvement in matters that would cause large-cap governance experts to jump out of their respective seats. A good example of that unique need for greater board involvement is the process of meeting with investors in advance of a financing.

Large-cap companies, because of balance sheet strength, often have the ability to opportunistically control the timing of financings, are well known to the investor community, have very actively traded stocks, and are extensively covered by equity research analysts. In addition management teams are typically seasoned public company veterans. Therefore, financings, and preparations for investor meetings more specifically, are predominantly (if not exclusively) management's province.

On the other hand, for most small-cap companies, financings are often time-sensitive matters of life and death, companies are not widely known, and stocks often aren't actively traded or covered extensively by research analysts (if at all). Furthermore, management teams are often quite new to public company stewardship, corporate finance, and the capital markets. Consequently, it's incumbent upon small-cap boards to be highly involved in all the elements of a financing from start to finish, including preparing for and conducting investor meetings.

Investor meetings are a considerably more integral part of financings for small-cap companies than they are for larger companies because in situations in which companies are nascent and riskier, investors are betting as much or more on management than anything else. Moreover, because small-cap companies typically aren't well known, investor meetings are often introductions of both company and management to investors. And since management experience in the small-cap ecosystem can be highly variable, the results of investor meetings can be binary in the absence of board supervision.

PRELIMINARY BOARD DETERMINATIONS

Given the heightened role that investor meetings play in the successful outcome of small-cap financings, boards need to make some preliminary determinations about how involved they will be in assisting management in preparing for investor meetings.

1. *Prior financings.* An obvious place the board can look to gain some clarity about the relative need for its involvement is the manner in which prior financings were handled (if it's the same management team). That is, if the management team has been successful previously in a number of financings[1] and has demonstrated the ability to present the company to investors with aplomb,[2] then the board might feel that minimal input is required.

2. *Inexperienced management team.* If management doesn't have any financing track record with the company, or has minimal previous public company financing experience then the board might make the determination that it needs to be more involved than less.

> TIP
>
> A scenario that's quite common in the small-cap realm is where the CEO has done an expert job in founding and growing the business, but, for any number of reasons, doesn't inspire confidence among investors. These situations are challenging inasmuch as the company is identified with the CEO and vice versa. Boards need to maintain objectivity with respect to the CEO's presentation skills, regardless of their title, and importance to the business. The **key point** here is that if the CEO is better at running the business than at investor presentations, then the board should strongly consider having other senior management personnel be the primary liaison with the investor community for financings and beyond.

GOOD STARTING POINT

When a board determines that it needs to be either more or less involved in management's preparations to meet with investors for a financing, having management run through a mock investor presentation with the board is a good idea for a number of reasons:

1. *The basics.* As institutional investors and investment bankers will attest, you can have a great company and a great person presenting the company, but if the presentation itself is substandard, then it's simply an opportunity lost. Important things for the board to focus on are: (a) the presentation should be comparatively succinct; it shouldn't be longer than 20 to 25 minutes; (b) the presentation needs to be geared toward the sophistication level of the audience; (c) the presentation needs to be in good English and factual beyond reproach; (d) the tone should be confident without being too "salesy;" (e) the board together with counsel should make sure that nothing in the presentation violates Regulation FD (the SEC's prohibition against selective disclosure of material nonpublic information adopted in 2000); and (f) when in doubt, leave out forward-looking information like multi-year projections since most experienced investors disregard them at best, and they can make the company look unsophisticated.[3]

TIP

For companies whose value proposition is inextricably linked to intellectual property, there is a predisposition toward highly technical investor presentations. What many small-cap officers and directors fail to appreciate is that even highly specialized investment funds often don't have portfolio managers that understand the technology or science as well as the officers and directors. The **key point** here is that speaking over investors' heads is almost worse than not speaking to them at all because if they can't understand the company, then they know no one else will be able to understand the company either. Therefore, encourage management to aim for a comparatively low common denominator with investor presentations, and then use the Q & A time to fine-tune the level of sophistication.

2. *Banker input.* It's a good idea for the board to review the prospective investor presentation with management before any banker input is provided because it's easier thereafter for the board to appreciate and evaluate the changes being suggested by the bankers. Sometimes, the input from bankers will be limited to style and formatting, but often bankers will recommend changing the overall tone, nomenclature, business description, statistics, and so on. The suggested changes should be carefully discussed with management and counsel.

TIP

Referring to every firm that assists small-cap companies with financings as an "investment bank" can be misleading, especially to directors with minimal small-cap experience. That is, many investment banks in small-cap finance would be more accurately referred to as "finders." Unlike full-service investment banks with investment banking, equity capital markets, research, and so on that provide comprehensive financing resources and support, many small-cap focused investment banks are niche broker-dealers whose role is predominantly to set up physical or telephonic investors meetings with companies to facilitate financings. To be clear, this is not in any way to impugn the value that finders bring to the small-cap ecosystem. Quite the contrary. They perform a critical role in matching companies with prospective investors. The **key point** here is that small-cap boards need to be very clear about what type of firm they've retained and what type of assistance will be forthcoming with respect to preparing management for the investor meetings. Small-cap boards often wrongfully assume that banks they've retained are going to "do it all," when in reality those firms offer fewer services than was envisioned.

INPUT ON INVESTOR SELECTION

While investment banks (and finders) are paid to, among other things, arrange meetings with investors likely to have an interest in the company, small-cap companies are often too deferential in this regard. More specifically, directors should make sure that management is receiving clear communication from the bankers about the financing strategy and how each prospective investor meeting fits within that strategy. Bankers should be able to succinctly set forth: (1) what types of companies the investors typically invest in; (2) the typical amount they invest; (3) whether the investors have investments in peer companies; and (4) other material anecdotal information about the investors historic likes and dislikes. This frank, open communication regarding investor meetings is perhaps even more critical in situations like follow-ons where extensive investor meetings can result in material expenditures of management time.

TIP

The strategy associated with and the process of planning investor meetings is another "trust but verify" situation for small-cap directors. That is, officers and directors don't have to take the words of investment bankers regarding the relative merits of meeting with some investors as opposed to others. Just as deal term data are publicly available, so too is an extensive amount of information about investors' past investments directly into public companies (and their current portfolios if they disclose them to the SEC quarterly on Form 13F). Directors should encourage management to carefully scrutinize proposed investor meetings and propose alternate investors who appear to be good prospects based on prior financings data. Not only does this ensure that time is well spent in connection with financings, but it also sends an important message to the company's bankers that the company is an informed, interested consumer of banking services.

AVOIDING COMMON MISTAKES

Where appropriate, small-cap boards should consider advising officers with limited experience, so that they can avoid making common mistakes while meeting with investors:

1. *Comportment.* As discussed earlier, there is considerably more focus in the small-cap realm on the CEO than perhaps there is in larger company settings because nascent companies by nature are more dependent on the vision, will, and execution of the CEO. Therefore, boards should spend time with less experienced CEOs and explain to them that they should maintain a balanced, steady demeanor at investor meetings, tone of the meetings notwithstanding. Less experienced management teams often take rigorous investor questioning personally and too easily lose their cool. Alternatively, collegial investor meetings occasionally bait the less experienced officer into speaking off message. It's important for boards to instill in less experienced management that veteran institutional investors have literally met with hundreds (if not more)

CEOs, and while management's comportment might not meaningfully help the company's ability to transact a financing, it can definitely hurt those chances.

TIP

Because of the heightened importance of CEOs in smaller public companies, small-cap investors' scrutiny of a CEO's background can often border on forensic. Consequently, boards should make sure that management's bios are factual and thorough. Regarding thoroughness, easily the most common mistake made in CEO bios is summarizing experience rather than providing precise positions and company names. Nothing scares away institutional investors right out of the gate more than something like, "Mr. Smith has had senior operating roles for the last 12 years with large commercial banks. Prior to that, Mr. Smith was the CFO of a midsized robotics company." The **key point** here is that small-cap investors are often betting substantially on the CEO, and they are less likely to even consider that bet if the CEO's background description creates more questions than it provides answers.

2. *PowerPoint.* There are a considerable number of institutional investors who loathe sitting through computerized investor presentations. Unfortunately, there are nearly an equal number of small-cap CEOs who are virtually incapable of making compelling investor presentations *without* computers. Therefore, directors should strongly encourage management to practice making presentations about the company without a computer.

3. *"I Don't Know."* Even experienced officers can benefit from a friendly reminder that these three words are often demonstrably better than the alternative when meeting with

investors. Institutional investors don't expect management teams to know everything about the company or the industry. Less experienced CEOs should be reminded of this by the board. Management teams often underestimate how good institutional investors are at listening and taking notes. Therefore, speculative, imprecise, or rambling answers not only routinely fail to impress, but they also might well be turned against the company for the investors' benefit.

TIP

One of the oldest "tricks" in the arsenals of experienced small-cap investors is to encourage a CEO who talks too much to keep talking. The benefit to meeting with CEOs in advance of financings who don't speak carefully is that savvy institutional investors can incorporate the information they glean from too much talk into a term sheet to their own advantage. For example, if a CEO speculates (within the confines of Regulation FD) that he'd be shocked if the company didn't turn the inventory much more rapidly by the same time next year, the investor can craft a milestone covenant to that effect in the convertible note proposed to the company. The company will then be in a difficult spot in negotiating that particular term; that is, it either has to admit that the CEO wasn't speaking carefully or accurately (not a good thing), or it might need to agree to a burdensome covenant (also not a good thing). The **key point** here is that small-cap CEOs can always benefit from a friendly reminder from the board to stick to the facts in investor meetings; if investors don't like the facts, then they aren't the right investors.

4. *Regulation FD.* A close corollary to speaking too much is saying the wrong things. While FD is now well engrained in corporate discourse in all sizes of public companies, there are still two

situations in the small-cap ecosystem where FD is often skirted: (a) less experienced management teams; and (b) experienced management teams of companies that are in dire situations. There are two things that small-cap directors can do to help ensure that FD is obeyed in the investor meeting context. First, they can, together with counsel, simply remind management prior to the beginning of investor meetings to make sure that the spirit and letter of FD are upheld. And second they can underscore a point that's easily lost in the investor meeting context; that is, the vast majority of institutional investors are far from appreciative of disclosures made in contravention of FD.

5. *Investor diligence.* While investor meetings in anticipation of a financing are principally intended to educate investors about the company, they are also unique opportunities for companies to size up investors. For example, were the investors professional, were they prepared, did they have material domain expertise, and did they ask insightful questions? These observations are critical for two widely overlooked reasons: (a) the comportment of the investors can provide material insight into the fund's investment modality; and (b) it's not just long-biased investors who attend investor meetings for financings.[4]

TIP

Even seasoned directors sometimes fail to appreciate that in the small-cap ecosystem there are investors and there are financiers. Unlike investors, a financier's business model is predicated on making a modest return on risk capital invested directly in the company, whether the company does well or poorly. While investors use domain expertise and extensive diligence to bet on the longer-term trajectories (up or down) of companies, the tools of the financier are a blend of investment structure and capital markets savvy.

Management teams that are paying attention during small-cap investor meetings will likely notice that some meetings are characterized by material domain expertise and insightful questions about the company's science, technology, products, services, competitors, and the like, while other meetings are nearly devoid of these issues. The **key point** here is that if virtually no insightful questions are asked of the company during an investor meeting and the party proffers a financing term sheet to the company soon after the meeting, the company is dealing with financiers not investors. The routine failure of small-cap companies to make that distinction is significant because officers and directors wrongfully assume that any party that invests capital directly into the company is a "partner." Financiers, though, are not in the "partnering" business; they are, instead, in the "make a modest, replicable return on their capital" business. This material disconnect plays out regularly when, for example, small-cap companies expend precious time and energy asking their "partners" for more capital or contractual concessions (e.g., waiving covenants, penalties, etc.), only to be mystified by repeated refusals to cooperate.

To be clear, financiers play a critical role in the small-cap ecosystem (especially in financing troubled smaller companies). It's critical for officers and directors to understand what type of entities they are dealing with, and what those entities do for a living. For well-prepared management teams, these realizations should start in the investor meetings.

Notes

1. As discussed in Chapter 2 "successful financings" doesn't just mean that the company was able to sell stock. Rather, successful means that the company was able to attract financing terms that were equal to or less dilutive than peers.

2. Since there isn't any objective way to determine this, boards needs to base such determinations upon anecdotal information supplied by bankers and investors.

3. The inclusion of multi-year revenue projections in investor presentations represents a material disconnect between the way management and institutional investors think. When management includes projections in investor presentations, they do so because it expresses their confidence in the business and induces investors to think beyond the stage the company is at now to what "could be." From a sophisticated investor's standpoint though, rarely if ever have they seen companies actually achieve their multi-year projections. Consequently, institutional investors are more inclined to view the projections as unsubstantiated optimism as opposed to confidence. The best rule of thumb is that forward-looking revenue and profitability outlooks in investor presentations should be limited to whatever companies have previously stated in their regulatory filings and/or press releases.

4. In the context, for example, of a follow-on, investors who have previously sold the company's stock short often participate in investor meetings in order to get allocated stock in the follow-on, which will facilitate the investors covering their short sale without pushing the price up. While this is a good result for the investor who is short, it's a bad result for the company because long-biased investors aren't getting stock, and the short investor is not covering by buying stock in the open market.

CHAPTER 5

NEGOTIATING

DEFINITIVE TERMS

Leveling the Playing Field with Investors

Key considerations for directors:

- Small-cap investors enjoy a material advantage over companies when negotiating financings.
- Regardless of the structure, boards need to make sure that they understand pricing mechanisms, which are often not as straightforward as they seem.
- Convertible instruments have a litany of provisions that might seem innocuous but that require board scrutiny.
- What companies thought they agreed to in a "term sheet" might look very different once the definitive deal documents arrive.

- Officers and directors need to involve counsel and auditors in financing negotiations every step of the way.

Common mistakes to avoid:

- Before small-cap boards walk away from financings because of a problem with price, they should first analyze the veracity of their stock price.
- If directors can't understand the terms of a financing, the company should walk away.
- Directors should advise officers to exercise care with respect to the type of information communicated to investors while under a non-disclosure agreement.

Whe it comes to negotiating small-cap financings, it is not a level playing field for many companies—not even close. While most companies have experience transacting a handful of financings, there are institutional investors (and their hyperspecialized attorneys) who have undertaken *hundreds*. And, as mentioned in Chapter 1, small-cap companies sometimes exacerbate this disadvantage by failing to retain appropriately expert counsel.

Though no single chapter, or book for that matter, can cover every issue that requires the board's focus, the purpose of this chapter is to highlight the places where small-cap companies typically get outfoxed when financings evolve from theory to reality.

Before delving into the granular issues deserving special consideration, it's important first to discuss three critical preliminary issues that are the root cause of many of the mistakes made by small-cap officers and directors when negotiating financings:

1. *Recalcitrance versus reality.* It doesn't take much for many small-cap financing negotiations to devolve into equal parts theater and sporting event, where acumen is regrettably overcome by ego. Particularly with more diminutive small-cap companies that have fewer alternatives, officers and directors often can have visceral reactions to how penal financing terms appear when they are put on paper. From the company's point of view, the terms often seem usurious and somehow disconnected from the promise of the company. While, from the institutional investor's standpoint, the terms match how they objectively assess risk. In the heat of the situation, it's often easy for small-cap boards to lose sight of the fact that especially for smaller, less actively traded issuers, the companies need the investors a lot more than the investors need the companies. Though frustration and reticence are understandable, boards should consider diffusing the situation with data. The **key point** here is that once officers and directors are satisfied that they are getting

competitive financing terms, they need to put ego aside and do what's right for the shareholders—use the growth capital as effectively as possible and strive to evolve the company to a point where if it needs to raise capital again, the results will be far less dilutive.

2. *The valuation "myth."* For larger public companies, the daily stock price is an indication of how the market values them at any moment in time. That value is supported by sometimes dozens of equity research reports, copious amounts of public information, and anywhere from dozens of millions to billions of dollars of trading each day to support that valuation. On the other hand, there are many hundreds of small-cap companies that have a handful of equity research reports, if any, scant amounts of publicly available information, and sometimes as little as thousands of dollars of trading each day[1] to support the stock price. The stock price for scores of small-cap companies isn't really a valuation at all. Rather it's more of an advisory figure. Why? Because the reality for many small-cap companies is that if a shareholder sought to sell a comparatively small amount of stock on any given day,[2] the stock price could swoon *dramatically* downward because of illiquidity. Therefore, the stock "price" only represents a real valuation for these companies if no one actually tries to sell any appreciable amount of stock. Hence valuations are sometimes not valuations at all. For a culture that's attuned to the notion that stock price equals the market's valuation, this small-cap valuation myth is not only counterintuitive, but it's also a hard pill to swallow. The **key point** here is that when negotiating a financing, many small-cap officers and directors need to keep valuation in perspective lest something that might be somewhat illusory becomes an impediment to securing much needed growth capital.

3. *Complexity.* The smaller and less actively traded a small-cap company is, the higher the likelihood that its financings will be more complex than they are for larger, more actively traded companies because investors utilize more intricate structures to offset heightened risk and illiquidity. Not every financing that's challenging for officers and directors to understand is necessarily bad for shareholders, but, it's not a bad bet for directors to make that complexity and "shareholder friendly" tend to be inversely proportional. The **key point** here is that if the officers, directors, counsel, and auditors can't readily understand the terms of a financing, then the board should strongly consider another route. Though this sounds like an intuitive admonishment, it's unfortunate how often small-cap companies undertake financings that they simply don't understand.

TIP

When faced with terms or a structure that the board doesn't understand, directors should consider asking prospective investors to provide hypothetical examples in order to clarify things. There are two benefits to this underutilized approach: (1) examples have a way of nullifying unfamiliar terms and legalese and of making otherwise complex financing elements more readily understood; and (2) if the investors can't provide an easy-to-understand hypothetical or are resistant to doing so, the board should reevaluate whether the investors are a good fit for the company.

SPECIAL PRICING CONSIDERATIONS

Though financing scenarios are infinite, there are certain pricing considerations which are recurring in the small-cap ecosystem.

RESTRICTED COMMON STOCK, CONVERTIBLE
INSTRUMENTS, AND EQUITY LINES

When negotiating pricing with respect to these financing structures, officers and directors should consider exercising extra care with respect to certain issues.

Volume Weighted Average Price (VWAP)

- Many officers and directors are unfamiliar with the term VWAP. A VWAP is not something calculated by companies or investors. Rather it is typically a calculation that is taken from Bloomberg's daily financial data. A VWAP is often used in connection with pricing small-cap financings because the financings can involve stocks that aren't actively traded. When stocks are not actively traded, the daily closing bid price can misrepresent what the stock has been trading for during the whole of the trading day. This is because a purchase or sale proximate to the close of trading in an inactively traded stock can raise or lower the price dramatically. Therefore, a VWAP more accurately depicts where the lion's share of the trading volume valued that stock on any given day.

- Though a VWAP is often a more accurate metric to use when pricing small-cap financings, officers and directors need to read the proposed pricing provisions carefully to understand what price is actually being suggested. For example, "the average VWAP for the five trading days immediately preceding the closing day" is not the same thing as "the average of the daily VWAPs for the five trading days immediately preceding the closing day." The former is just a number taken from Bloomberg which computes the VWAP for the five-day period, while the latter is an average of each of the daily VWAPs. These can lead to different numbers, and so it should be assumed that whichever the investors are selecting is the number most beneficial to them. Moreover, typically the investors will select different pricing periods to get the lowest recent trading days.

Pricing Periods and Variable Priced Conversions

- Any time there is a pricing period calculation or a convertible instrument that has a variable or floating conversion feature, officers and directors have to read those provisions with counsel very carefully. As discussed above, it's always a good idea to request a hypothetical from the investors to make sure that the parties are on the same pages with respect to how the pricing feature works.

- Companies should consider negotiating measures to ensure that investors can't be trading in the company's stock (or undertaking any other actions that can influence the price of the company's stock) during any pricing periods or variable priced conversions, lest the investors attempt to influence the stock price to their benefit.

- With respect to any variable priced instruments, companies should strongly consider having a floor price beneath which sales or conversions cannot occur.

Convertible Note Pricing

- If a company is particularly interested in mitigating dilution (i.e., keeping the conversion discount to a minimum), an original issue discount (OID) could be considered. An OID essentially sells the note to investors at a discount to par (e.g., the investors pay $5 million for a note, but the company needs to pay them back that principal plus an additional sum equal to the discount to par in addition to accrued interest). Since the investors are receiving a financial benefit from the OID, some investors might be more amenable to trade that benefit for a higher conversion price. Prior to considering this, officers and directors should discuss it with counsel and auditors so that they will understand the impact on the company's accounting, and so on.

Interest and Dividends

- Officers and directors should assume that when it comes to interest rates and dividends, investors do their best to try to get the highest rates possible. The best defense for companies is data. A review of recent peer financings will be instructive as to whether the interest or dividends sought are consistent with what other similar companies have agreed to or not agreed to.

FOLLOW-ONS, RDS, AND CMPOS

When negotiating pricing with respect to these financing structures, officers and directors should consider exercising extra care with respect to certain issues:

- While there is, of course, nothing wrong at all with a board doing its best to get the least dilutive pricing possible, small-cap boards need to balance that interest with a realization that institutional investors are very much aware of when they are being "top-ticked." That is, companies that seek to opportunistically price these financings to coincide with spikes in stock price or 52-week high prices will receive material pushback from investors, who will be more focused on the last price where the stock traded for an extended period of time. Therefore, small-cap boards need to be realistic about pricing under these circumstances.

- Moreover, boards should also be aware that sometimes the highest possible price where a follow-on, RD, or CMPO could conceivably be priced isn't always the best price for the board to pursue. Often, the company might be able to have better-quality investors and better postfinancing results if the deal is priced below the highest price the market will bear.[3]

> TIP
>
> In situations where a company transacts an RD or a CMPO with warrants, small-cap officers and directors often can't understand why the day the financing is announced the stock price often trades below the offering price. A question that is often asked is, "Why are the investors selling the stock they just bought at $9 for $8.50?" The short answer is fund management accounting. As discussed in Chapter 2, there are funds that ascribe an immediate value to warrants received in conjunction with a financing based on Black-Scholes. Therefore, when warrants are issued in connection with an RD or a CMPO, the warrant valuation might, from an accounting perspective, decrease the price the investors effectively paid for the stock. Therefore, if in the above example, the warrants reduced the investors' effective purchase price to $8, then they are actually still making money by selling stock at $8.50, notwithstanding the $9 deal price.

Options and Warrants

Following are a couple of pricing thoughts for boards to consider regarding options and warrants:

- *Options.* For small-cap companies that are considering restricted common stock, convertible preferred, or convertible note financings, in particular, and also have options listed for trading, the ability for investors to hedge the downside risk in the options market might provide the company with the ability to negotiate smaller discounts when selling restricted stock. This is, of course, not something the investors are going to volunteer to do, but it's something that the company can possibly use to its benefit during price negotiations.

- *Warrants.* Exercise pricing for warrants might seem arbitrary to some companies, but it is often reliant upon the Black-Scholes modeling employed by the investors. For example, depending on the volatility of a stock and the negotiated term of the warrant, investors may or may not have a high degree of sensitivity to the strike price. Data can certainly help companies as they seek to negotiate warrant pricing. Directors should make sure that auditors are engaged in the process to provide advice concerning the impact of prospective warrant pricing on Generally Accepted Accounting Principles ("GAAP") accounting.

SPECIAL CONVERTIBLE INSTRUMENT[4] CONSIDERATIONS

Convertible instruments in small-cap finance range from banal to mind-numbingly complex, but there are common features that are critical for officers and directors to understand.

Term (for Repayment)

Small-cap boards sometimes employ insufficient analyses regarding whether the term being proposed by investors for repayment is appropriate for the company's situation. As discussed in Chapter 2, boards should certainly not gloss over the length of the term with the notion that it can simply be renegotiated down the road. This is not a strategy that will likely benefit the company's shareholders.

Ownership "Blockers"

When negotiating convertible instruments, investors often request a provision that states that the investors at no time will be able to convert sufficient amounts of the instrument so that they own more than 9.99 percent of the issued and outstanding common stock of the company. Small-cap officers and directors often don't understand the need for this ownership "blocker" from the investors' standpoint, and the importance of adhering to it if the agreement ultimately contains that provision. The reason why investors require a 9.99 percent blocker is that once an investor goes over that ownership percentage, the investor is considered an insider under the federal securities laws and is not able to trade the stock freely. Given the criticality of the blockers to investors who seek the provision, the company needs to establish internal controls to ensure adherence to the provision.

MANDATORY CONVERSION

Some convertible instruments provide the ability for the company, under certain circumstances, to force the investors to convert the instruments into common stock. The notion of being able to force the investors to convert (and thus expunge the convertible instrument from the balance sheet) is understandably attractive to small-cap companies. Unfortunately, many officers and directors don't pay close enough attention when negotiating these provisions only to find that the company's ability to force conversion is extremely limited. Therefore, if the ability to force conversion is important to the company, it should pay careful attention to the preconditions. Typical conditions include, but are not limited to, the need for an effective registration statement covering the common stock underlying the convertible instrument, the need for the stock to have traded a certain daily dollar volume for some prescribed period of time, the maintenance of the company's exchange listing, and the need for the stock to have achieved some percentage premium to the exercise price for some prescribed period of time. In other words, investors attempt to make sure that the company can't "put" the stock to the investors in circumstances where the investors wouldn't be able to sell the stock profitably. The board should make sure that the preconditions are reasonable under the circumstance before agreeing to the same.

BUY-IN

Any time an investor converts an instrument into common stock (or exercises a warrant), the company is often contractually obligated to deliver the corresponding number of registered, freely tradeable common shares to the investor within three trading days. The reason for this is that investors often sell the shares they are converting or exercising prior to actually receiving them,[5] and have three days to deliver those shares and settle the trade (sometime referred to as a "T + 3 settlement"). If the investor is unable to settle the trade within three trading days because the company didn't deliver the shares in a timely manner, then the investor will be forced by the settling broker to go into the marketplace and purchase the shares and deliver them (a "buy-in"). If the investors would have made a profit of $2 per share if the company delivered the shares in a timely way but because of the buy-in the investors made a profit of only $1 per share, then buy-in provisions in most convertible instruments (and warrants) make the company liable for the delta. Since thousands if not millions of shares can sometimes be at issue, buy-in liability can be anywhere from unpleasant to business-ending for small-cap companies. Therefore, if any financing documents contain buy-in provisions, it's critical that boards make sure that management, counsel, auditors, and transfer agents all understand the timelines associated with share delivery and the repercussions for failures to conform to those timelines.

Prepayment

Having paid insufficient attention to prepayment provisions during negotiations, many small-cap boards are dismayed when the company attempts to prepay a convertible instrument and are required to pay the investors an appreciable penalty (sometimes as much as 25 percent). If the company believes that there is a reasonable chance that it will prepay the obligation before its term, then it should consider negotiating the prepayment penalties more strenuously. Moreover, convertible notes occasionally also have interest "make-whole" provisions which require the company to pay investors all the interest the investors would have received if the notes went to term in the event the note is prepaid. Given the combined austerity of prepayment penalties and interest make-whole provisions, officers and directors need to discuss them and factor them into the cost of capital.

AMORTIZING NOTES

Also known as self-liquidating notes, this feature requires the company to begin making mandatory periodic principal repayment until the principal of the note is repaid. This is often appealing to investors because it is seen as mitigating the scenario where the note goes to term, and only then is it clear that the company can't repay the principal.

Sometimes amortizing notes are payable to the investors in stock in lieu of cash, at the election of the company. This is often viewed by officers and directors as an attractive alternative since it can preserve much needed cash. But frequently the ability to pay in stock is available only under painstakingly enumerated circumstances (akin to mandatory conversion provisions discussed earlier). Therefore, if the ability to pay in stock is important to the company, then the board should make sure that management and counsel are focused on carefully negotiating this, for example: (1) when and how notice is provided to the investors that the company intends to make a payment in stock instead of cash; (2) what pricing mechanism will be used to determine how many shares will be paid; and (3) whether the investors are permitted to trade the company's stock during any of the pricing periods.

TIP

Any time the company envisions making an amortization payment of stock in lieu of cash (or in any conversion, exercise, or "put" situation), the company needs to be very careful not to provide the investors with material, nonpublic information that would prevent them from selling until the information is either public or becomes immaterial. Forgetting for the moment whether such a disclosure violates Regulation FD, the more salient issue for purposes of the intended share delivery is that it forecloses the investors' ability to sell the stock and likely forecloses the stock delivery altogether. While companies, of course, need to comply with Regulation FD at all times,

> the **key point** here is that they need to be especially careful what is
> said to investors in and around the time periods where freely trade-
> able shares are being delivered to them.

SECURITY

If a convertible note being negotiated requires security interest in assets or
seniority in the capital structure, officers and directors need to make sure
that counsel is sufficiently involved to obviate agreeing to something that's
untenable or breaches other agreements. As discussed in Chapter 1, issues
like this should be addressed long before financing terms are negotiated, but
unfortunately they often come up at the last second in small-cap financings.

MISCELLANEOUS TERMS

There are a number of provisions that are often suggested by investors
that officers and directors should carefully consider. These include:

- *New indebtedness.* Investors in convertible instruments often seek
  to have companies agree that they will get prior written approval
  of the investors prior to incurring any additional indebtedness.
  Boards should make sure officers carefully consider whether this
  proscription provides the company with sufficient flexibility,
  inasmuch as investors aren't typically receptive to waiving this once
  it's memorialized in an agreement.

- *Reverse stock split.* It's quite common for investors in convertible
  instruments to demand that during the term of the instrument, the
  company will be forbidden from doing a reverse stock split unless
  prior written approval is granted by the investors. This is something
  that officers and directors need to consider carefully, inasmuch
  as companies might also have other contractual obligations that
  contain austere penalties if, for example, a senior exchange listing is
  lost. At the same time, it's also important for boards to understand
  why investors typically demand this concession. The preponderance

of small-cap reverse stock splits are unattractive to shareholders, at least in the near term. This is discussed in greater depth in Part Two.

- *Equity lines or variable priced instruments.* Investors in convertible instruments typically forbid companies from entering into equity lines or variable priced instruments while the convertible instrument is still outstanding. Officers and directors need to exercise care in agreeing to this because such a prohibition certainly can diminish funding alternatives going forward. Investors, for their part, typically demand it because equity lines and variable priced instruments can often have a deleterious impact on overall interest in a company's stock which could be harmful to the investors' interests.

- *Rights of participation or first refusal.* In exchange for the risk associated with investing in convertible instruments, investors typically request the right to be able to participate in future financings. For example, if this investment goes well, the investors want the ability to do it again. Though there isn't anything sinister about this in theory, small-cap companies that do a poor job of vetting investors prior to financings can pay a steep price for this by not only doing one financing with a challenging investor group, but also agreeing to be joined at the hip with this group going forward. There are more than a handful of small-cap companies that have suffered dramatically from being tied to investors with poor reputations in the marketplace. This underscores the importance of doing due diligence on investors under consideration, banker admonitions notwithstanding.

SPECIAL REGISTRATION RIGHTS CONSIDERATIONS

Though small-cap companies regularly enter into registration rights agreements with investors, officers and directors should focus on these common provisions.

LIQUIDATED DAMAGES

Registration rights agreements typically provide investors with the right to receive liquidated damages for the the company's failure to, among other things, file the registration statement by a certain time, and have it be declared effective by the SEC by a certain time. With respect to filing by a certain time, companies are uniquely in control over when and if a registration statement can be filed in a timely way. It's important for small-cap officers and directors to be clear that with the exception of responding to the government's requests for information in a timely fashion, companies have absolutely no control over when a registration statement will be declared effective, regardless of what counsel might say. Therefore, as it pertains to evaluating the liquidated damages set forth in the proposed registration rights agreement, boards should consider discussing the following questions (with counsel included): (1) Are the liquidated damages requested in the registration rights agreement consistent with what peers have recently agreed to? (2) Are there any reasons why the board, management, and counsel believe that the company can't file the registration statement within the period set forth in the proposed registration rights agreement? (3) Are there any extenuating reasons why the board, management, and counsel believe that the registration statement will not be declared effective within the time limit permitted? The board and counsel should also discuss when the investors will be able to resell stock in the market with or without an effective registration statement under the amended provision of Rule 144; that is, depending upon the applicable holding periods under Rule 144 for the company, the investors will be able to sell stock in the marketplace at some point after which liquidated damages should be less applicable.

NUMBER OF SHARES

As discussed in Chapter 1, officers and directors need to make sure that they are on the same page concerning how many shares can be registered. In order to do this, they must make sure that they are being advised by counsel who is highly knowledgeable about the relevant regulatory issues.

SPECIAL EQUITY LINE CONSIDERATIONS

Equity lines are notionally straightforward, but equity line documentation can be complex and deserving of close scrutiny by officers and directors.

COMMITMENT SHARES

It's not uncommon for equity line investors to seek commitment shares; that is, an upfront payment of common stock in exchange for the equity line commitment that is typically nonrefundable. The investor rationale for this is that since most equity lines can be cancelled at the unilateral option of the company, the commitment shares offset the lost opportunity cost of a prematurely cancelled line. Officers and directors faced with weighing this provision should, at the least, consider requesting that if the shares are issued, the investors have to agree in return not to sell the shares until some date certain or not at all during the pendency of the equity line. That is, since equity line pricing is determined by contractually determined discounts to then market prices, a sale of any or all of the commitment shares could result in more dilutive pricing; i.e., commitment shares have the potential to create a conflict of interest.

COVENANTS

Other than the company's need to register the common stock underlying the equity line (and keep it registered) and the proscription against any act or omission by the company that could result in the investors being restricted from trading during a pricing period, the board should be circumspect of any additional covenants requested by equity line investors. Equity lines provide the ability for companies to electively "put" stock to investors when they see fit; therefore, any additional, material restrictions diminish the main attraction to equity lines—flexibility.

TERMINATION

It's worth reiterating that, as discussed in Chapter 2, officers and directors should pay close attention to the termination provisions of equity lines; the provisions should be simple and unambiguous.

SPECIAL ATM CONSIDERATIONS

Like equity lines, ATM's are notionally straightforward, but have unique issues.

CONFLICTS

When negotiating an ATM, officers and directors should make sure to confirm that the potential conflicts of interest discussed in Chapter 2 (market making, proprietary trading, etc.) are not only understood but largely mitigated.

TIMING

Boards should also pay special attention to the provisions that set forth when the ATM facility may not be utilized, and they should make sure to discuss with officers whether those provisions will affect the company's plans.

SPECIAL RD AND CMPO CONSIDERATIONS— ABILITY TO TRADE

One of the central benefits to investors of investing in an RD or a CMPO is that they are able to sell their stock whenever they wish after the financing is publicly announced. The only impediment to this ability is if the investors feel that they are in possession of material, nonpublic information. Since RDs and CMPOs are marketed privately, management teams occasionally speak more "freely" than they should, and would otherwise do, for example, in a follow-on environment.[6] From an investor's standpoint there are only two ways to address this situation: (1) the company either publicly announces the information before the financing is publicly announced; or (2) the investors won't invest. From a company standpoint, both of these outcomes aren't good, especially since there could be competitive reasons why disclosing information isn't advantageous to shareholders. Unfortunately, once the "horse leaves the barn" these negotiations rarely have good outcomes. Therefore, the best way to handle this situation is to make sure before the investor meetings that boards admonish management to stick 100 percent to public information only.

SPECIAL WARRANT CONSIDERATIONS

Warrants are a fact of life in small-cap finance, and deserve particular attention.

MISCELLANEOUS PROVISIONS
It's imperative that officers and directors, together with counsel, make sure that buy-in language, antidilution provisions, and change of control clauses are completely understood. Additionally, although small-cap companies often have a limited ability to negotiate the exclusion of these provisions, officers and directors should certainly consider attempting to minimize their impact.[7] This is especially true if the company is likely to undertake further financings or believes that a change of control might be likely because antidilution and change of control provisions often can be penal.

TRANSFERABILITY
Small-cap officers and directors (and counsel) often overlook warrant provisions dealing with transferability. Investors typically require that the warrants be transferable to third parties because occasionally they might seek to sell the warrant itself rather than exercise it. Especially when warrant coverage is material, companies need to be cognizant of the fact that as drafted many transferability clauses permit the transfer of warrants to, for example, competitors. Therefore, if directors are concerned about that possibility, they should encourage officers to negotiate those provisions carefully.

TIP

A universal consideration when negotiating small-cap financings is that officers and directors (and sometimes counsel as well) need to be prepared for the disparity between term sheets and definitive documentation. That is, a good percentage of the time, definitive documents are only loosely related to term sheets. This is not to say that fundamental terms are disingenuously changed in definitive documents; rather, it's what is added, not omitted, that is where the problems can lie. The **key point** here is that officers and directors need to trust but verify with respect to the deal documents, make sure they get clarification on provisions they don't understand, and make sure counsel is highly experienced at negotiating the type of financing envisioned.

Notes

1. There are many small-cap companies that go for days without ever opening for trading.

2. In order to make the point more objectively, if a stock can't substantially maintain its price without a shareholder being able to sell one-tenth of 1 percent (in dollars) of the nondiluted market capitalization in an orderly fashion over the course of one trading day, then the so-called "valuation" isn't terribly credible.

3. There are a couple of reasons for this: (1) institutional investor psychology is such that investors will often feel better about an investment where the pricing isn't at the highest possible end of the range; and (2) when deals are priced for perfection and perfection isn't the result, then the associated trading can be extra penal.

4. Most of the considerations set forth apply to convertible notes, but many similar issues arise in convertible preferred negotiations as well.

5. Small-cap officers and directors often don't understand completely why institutional investors do this. Investors typically sell shares they are exercising or converting immediately because they are exercising or converting for the purpose of selling shares. If they weren't intending to sell the shares, then there would be no reason to disturb the status quo.

6. Investors who are interested in learning about an RD or a CMPO typically sign nondisclosure agreements, wherein they agree not to either disclose to others that a company is contemplating an RD or a CMPO imminently, and they also agree not to trade in the company's stock until the financing either is transacted or is abandoned because of the passage of time. Having signed nondisclosure agreements, the investors still don't want to receive any information that at the time the financing is

announced isn't going to be made public or become immaterial. Though it's arguable that material, nonpublic information that is disclosed to investors under nondisclosure agreements might not be a violation of Regulation FD, the conundrum still exists; investors aren't going to invest in an RD or a CMPO if they are in possession of information that makes it unlawful for them to trade the stock.

7. For example, as discussed in Chapter 2, boards faced with the proposal of full-ratchet antidilution can try to negotiate weighted average antidilution instead (i.e., the latter is less dilutive), or boards can try to negotiate that the full-ratchet antidilution be removed after a period of time or upon achievement of a milestone that mitigates risk. Regarding the change of control provisions, many warrants require companies (or successors) to pay investors the full remaining Black-Scholes value of the warrants in cash if the company is acquired for cash or by a private company. Since such a payment could actually deter an acquisition that would otherwise benefit many shareholders, boards can try negotiating that the cash payments not be due the warrant holders if, perhaps, the acquisition consideration is above and beyond some percentage premium. The reality of warrant negotiations, though, is that if companies are in a position in which warrants are to be granted to begin with, then it's not likely that they have appreciable bargaining leverage with respect to some of the more objectionable provisions.

CHAPTER 6

AVOIDING COMMON POSTFINANCING MISTAKES

Common Postfinancing Mistakes

Key considerations for directors:

- Many small-cap financings don't end when the documents are signed.
- Directors might need to supervise how financings are communicated to investors.
- Directors need to ensure that processes are in place to administer financings postclosing.

Common mistakes to avoid:

- Especially with financings, small-cap companies often pay insufficient attention to the type of audience reading the press releases.
- Trying to "hide" dilutive financings in Form 8-K filings is a strategy more directors should question.
- Too many small-cap directors have no idea which elements of a financing could result in penalties and how material those penalties can be if postfinancing administration is poor.

G iven how important financings are to most small-cap companies, officers and directors tend to be hyperfocused on the relevant matters at hand from the beginning to the end. The mistake often made, though, is that many officers and directors consider the signing of definitive deal documents to be the end of the financing, whereas there are two additional steps that can be critical to a small-cap financing's success—publicly announcing the financing and complying with material terms.

The amount of focus required on announcing a financing and administering its salient terms is directly proportional to the complexity of the financing. For example, if a company sells 1 million common shares at a 5 percent discount to the previous day's closing bid price in an RD, there's obviously not a lot to explain or administer. However, if a company transacts a senior, secured, self-amortizing convertible note with an original issue discount and multiple tranches of callable warrants, then continued focus from officers and directors on explaining and administering the financing is critical. Considering that nearly 40 percent of small-cap financings in 2011 were more complex than selling restricted common stock and that nearly 80 percent of the financings required some postfinancing administration, there are a substantial number of officers and directors who need to exercise care not to prematurely focus on other matters.[1]

ANNOUNCING THE FINANCING

This is yet another example in which the people more familiar with governance at larger companies would be scratching their heads wondering why directors would need to be engaged in active dialogue with management about a press release that simply announces a financing. There are three reasons why small-cap directors should be more actively involved in management's public explanation of financings: (1) as discussed previously, there are scores of small-cap management teams with little experience in operating a public company and communicating with the Street; (2) the quality of small-cap investor relations firms is sufficiently disparate that boards need to trust advice but also need to verify it; and (3) since many small-cap companies are inactively traded, it takes a minimal amount of shareholder confusion to cause material share price erosion. Following are the most commonly made mistakes that small-cap directors should focus on with management.

AUDIENCE

Unlike larger public companies, many small-cap companies have predominantly retail shareholder bases; that is, institutional investors often provide financing, but the majority of investors who buy stock in the open market are often individuals.[2] Despite the statistically significant retail shareholder base, small-cap companies routinely craft press releases announcing complex financings for an audience they *don't* have. Press releases are often replete with sophisticated financial nomenclature and legalese to such an extent that even mutual fund managers might give pause. Nothing good ever comes from speaking over the heads of shareholders: it builds distrust; it creates more work for companies in answering scores of investor inquiries; and uncertainty in the capital markets historically breeds a predictable result—selling.

Why is this such a prevalent problem? Because, less experienced management teams lack sensitivity to the issue. They feel that the hard part of undertaking the financing is over, and so they outsource the crafting of press releases to those who share the lack of sensitivity to the issue. Although this is part of a larger issue that is discussed in greater detail in Part Two, company counsel and investor relations firms sometimes exacerbate this problem. The former are sometimes accustomed to working with larger companies and to communicating very formally; the latter sometimes are guilty of drafting releases that impress clients instead of artfully communicate the message to the company's audience. Therefore, the **key point** here is for directors to remind officers about the importance of clearly communicating the terms of the financing to the company's core audience and to make sure that the message is appropriately crafted for that audience.

FORM 8-K VERSUS PRESS RELEASE

Unless directed otherwise by a senior exchange, public companies typically have the choice of disclosing a financing through a Form 8-K filing or a press release (or both). Since many small-cap financings are highly dilutive to shareholders, companies sometimes opt for announcing financings via Form 8-K as opposed to a press release. The thinking in this regard is that a Form 8-K filing is likely to garner less attention than a press release—put bad news in a Form 8-K, and reserve press releases for better information. Investors understand the difference; it is uniformly understood in the investing community that when a company announces a financing via Form 8-K instead of a press release, the company knows it's not a great result for shareholders, and it's attempting the capital markets version of "hiding."

Small-cap directors should actively discuss with officers whether this is a prudent way to communicate with shareholders. While there are times when announcing a financing is clearly appropriate via Form 8-K,[3] officers and directors would do well to consider issuing press releases for financings on a case by case basis, dilution notwithstanding, so that the company can take ownership of the financing, clearly explain the terms, and move forward. The **key point** here is that announcing financings via Form 8-K is tantamount to deemphasizing material information, and investors are expressly cognizant of this, so small-cap directors should assist management with determining whether that's ultimately in the shareholders' interest.

LOST OPPORTUNITIES

It is, of course, prudent and necessary for companies to make sure that press releases are approved by counsel prior to their issuance. It's common in the small-cap ecosystem for companies to substantially defer to counsel for drafting financing-related press releases. The results, predictably, are dry, one-dimensional excerpts of the legalese contained in the financing documents, and here is a lost opportunity to communicate effectively with shareholders. More specifically, there are often "facts" that are just as important as the financial terms, which shareholders might not focus on but for highlighting them. For example, perhaps the same investors who previously financed the company have expressed confidence in the company by investing again,[4] perhaps the financing is less dilutive than previous financings, perhaps the pricing was at the market or even at a premium to the then market price, or perhaps some of the more onerous terms of a financing might be expunged if the company reaches certain milestones. The **key point** here is that small-cap directors should make sure that management, together with the company's professional service providers, are seeking to include relevant material facts in financing press releases so as not to waste an opportunity to communicate effectively with shareholders.

Context

Small-cap companies are subject to both macro and industry trends that impact valuations and the availability of growth capital more dramatically than for larger public companies. But shareholders (especially retail shareholders) might not always be aware of these issues, and many small-cap companies do a poor job of making them aware. Therefore, companies that are otherwise performing well compared to their peers[5] should certainly consider providing some relevant context to a dilutive financing when they announce this if outside factors materially contributed to the structure or terms of the financing. For example, in commenting on a financing, a CEO could cite references to other recent peer financings to illustrate that the company is not alone in facing financing headwinds. The **key point** here is that small-cap boards need to work together with management to make sure, where appropriate, that shareholders are provided with some context to enable them to better understand any relevant, material circumstances surrounding a financing.

EQUITY LINES AND ATMs

Although equity lines could well be appropriate financing choices for small-cap companies, they still suffer from historically pejorative connotations, and ATMs are still comparatively new in the small-cap realm. Therefore, directors need to work together with management to ensure that the press releases announcing these two structures don't make two common mistakes: (1) getting needlessly bogged down in pricing complexities and administration to the point where investors don't really understand why the structure is appropriate for the company's needs; and (2) failing to point out the favorable flexibility associated with the structures (e.g., unilaterally controlling when and how much stock is sold, and being able to terminate the structure whenever the company wishes).

ADMINISTERING THE FINANCING

It is a dramatically underappreciated fact of small-cap life that many financings have austere penalties[6] for companies that fail to strictly abide by the provisions set forth in the definitive deal documentation— penalties that under some circumstances can be business-ending. Consequently, small-cap directors have no choice but to understand any and all penalties contained in financing documents, and they need to take steps to ensure that officers also understand the penalties and are administratively prepared to abide by the financing's provisions.

RESTRICTED COMMON STOCK FINANCINGS

Although some financings can be transacted over the course of just several days, restricted common stock financings are good examples of how seemingly straightforward financings can have administrative hurdles that require board attention. Most restricted common stock financings have registration rights agreements, for example, that require companies to file registration statements by a particular deadline, respond to regulator requests within a certain period, and ultimately to have the registration statement declared effective by the SEC by a date certain. Especially for companies without meaningful experience in public company corporate finance, filing registration statements can be challenging, time-consuming exercises. Moreover, restricted common stock financings also typically contain provisions that require companies to remove restrictive legends from stock certificates once the registration statement is declared effective. This doesn't sound terribly difficult, but when a number of shareholders decide to sell stock simultaneously while the company is also trying to close its quarter or submit unrelated securities filings, it's understandable why unprepared companies can quickly run afoul of these provisions and begin to accumulate penalties. The **key point** here for small-cap directors is that it's a good idea to have counsel summarize any material requirements placed on the company by financings immediately upon closing them and to also clarify (with hypothetical examples) what situations could give rise to penalties. Thereafter, directors can work together with management to make sure that processes are in place to mitigate the possibility of breaching any of the financing provisions. Though these steps seem highly intuitive, it's instructive to note that very few small-cap boards ever undertake these precautions.

Convertible Financings

For most small-cap companies, there is no such thing as a simple convertible financing, inasmuch as pricing periods, voluntary conversions, involuntary conversions, amortizations, and so on create a blizzard of company deliverables for typically overworked, understaffed finance departments. Moreover, each of the deliverables is so meticulously drafted in convoluted legalese that company compliance can seem unattainable. However, small-cap companies routinely fail to take the necessary steps to prepare for administering these complex financings and this results in rampant penalties. More specifically, directors need to ensure that after the close of a convertible financing, there are a series of internal process meetings at which management, financing staff, counsel, and the company's transfer agent (if necessary) run through mock pricing, conversion, and amortization scenarios so that each constituency not only understands its role, but also all parties coalesce to produce deliverables within the time frames set forth in the financing documents. The **key point** here for directors is that the likelihood of incurring material penalties and liquidated damages after undertaking convertible financings is high if proper preparations aren't made, and it is naïve to plan on getting waivers from institutional investors to mitigate the risk.

POSTFINANCING COMMUNICATIONS WITH INVESTORS

Regardless of whether a company is performing well or poorly after a financing, many small-cap officers make a mistake by not taking the time to periodically meet personally with investors who have financed the company.

Although all such meetings are governed by the strictures of Regulation FD, the simple act of making an effort to travel to meet with investors face-to-face as opposed to over the telephone speaks volumes to investors about the company's commitment and integrity.

FINANCING IS THE EASY PART

To an appreciable degree, the financing is really the easy part, while the considerably harder part is constructively putting the capital to work in order to create value for shareholders. When companies accept growth capital from investors and management makes no effort to periodically spend time with them thereafter, it can negatively influence investors' perceptions of the company.

IN GOOD TIMES AND BAD

It's easy for management teams to take "victory laps" with investors when things are going well. What's often harder, and correspondingly more constructive, is to visit with investors when things aren't going well because investors not only want to be able to air their grievances directly with management, but they also want to gauge whether and to what extent the management team is affected by a performance problem.

BACK TO THE WELL

Last, but certainly not least, many small-cap companies are serial capital raisers, and the universe of institutional investors that invests directly in small-cap companies is finite. Therefore, management teams have a considerably better chance of cajoling repeat investments from investors when those investors feel that management is truthful, accountable, and present.

The **key point** here for small-cap directors is that postfinancing business performance doesn't, in and of itself, create good relationships with institutions that financed the company. Therefore, boards need to encourage management to visit with those institutions periodically, because the future availability of capital is an enterprise risk for small-cap companies that requires careful management.

Notes

1. According to PrivateRaise, approximately 40 percent of the small-cap financings in 2011 were convertible notes, convertible preferred, equity lines, or ATMs. Furthermore, when you add in restricted common stock financings, nearly 80 percent of the financings necessitated post-deal administration (e.g., pricing periods, cleaning restrictive legends off stock certificates, share conversions, etc.).

2. According to 2012 research from Keating Capital based on data from Capital IQ, for small-cap companies with market capitalizations between $100 to $300 million, for example, 42 percent of investors are individuals. For companies with less than $100 million market capitalizations, approximately 70 percent of investors are individuals.

3. If a company is simply drawing down on a previously announced equity line or an ATM facility, for example, then communicating this via Form 8-K will likely be viewed by the Street as reasonable.

4. Institutional investors typically won't agree to their names being included in financing press releases, but that needn't stop companies from pointing out the investors anonymously, where applicable. For example, companies can note that the same three institutional investors that participated in the company's last financing also participated in the current financing.

5. Companies, whether large or small, that are performing poorly are always going to undertake more dilutive financings than their peers, macro and industry trends notwithstanding.

6. Definitive deal documentation typically refers to penalties as "liquidated damages" in order to pass regulatory muster. Regardless of what they are called, they are penalties.

CHAPTER 7

WORKOUTS

Small-Cap Companies Versus Hedge Funds

Key considerations for directors:

- Small-cap companies are often at a disadvantage when negotiating against hedge funds to modify prior financing agreements.
- Understanding the business and psychology of hedge funds is a prerequisite.
- For many hedge funds, profit-and-loss impact of a financial modification is more important than what "might be best for shareholders."

Common mistakes to avoid:

- Planning on leniency from hedge funds when material financing terms are breached.
- Ignoring the business reasons behind affirmative and negative covenants.
- Seeking waivers for financing provisions without requisite understanding of and regard for the impact on a fund's profit and loss.

S mall-cap companies that transact enough financings—especially structured financings—will invariably be in a position where they need to negotiate with hedge funds in order to modify prior written financing agreements ("workouts"). The vast majority of small-cap officers and directors struggle mightily with workouts for two principal reasons: (1) hedge funds have leverage and experience on their side; and (2) many small-cap officers and directors aren't well-versed in the business and psychology of hedge funds.

Most small-cap workout situations arise when there is about to be a breach of a provision in definitive financing documents, or there has already been one. Whether anticipatory or reactive, small-cap companies tend to pursue similar tacks; that is, they either explain to hedge funds why waiving the breach would be in the best interests of shareholders, or they suggest some remediation.

As discussed in Chapter 4, the first time many small-cap officers and directors find out that hedge funds aren't necessarily "partners" is when companies seek a modification to complex financing documents only to be admonished in response that the contract is crystal clear as drafted, and what's in the best of interests of shareholders is neither here nor there.

After often being rebuffed on their waiver efforts, officers and directors then typically propose an array of concessions that they feel are creative and fair. Thereafter, they are typically even more confused when none of the proposed alternatives is even given so much as lip service by the hedge funds. It's almost like asking someone what his favorite color is, and he responds with a day of the week. This kind of thing happens almost every day in the small-cap ecosystem.

Ultimately, the biggest disconnect in these situations between small-cap companies and hedge funds is that officers and directors often fail to sufficiently understand one of the critical drivers of hedge fund behavior—fund management accounting. Hedge funds typically approach workout situations with the notion that any workout proposal from a company needs to be, at a minimum, neutral as to the fund's profit and loss (P&L) statement. But, given that the vast majority of small-cap officers and directors don't have buy-side experience and that hedge funds don't voluntarily disclose a lot of information about internal processes, it's not surprising that an inordinate amount of time is wasted each year with small-cap companies and hedge funds simply speaking past each other in workout situations.

HEDGE FUND ACCOUNTING

Hedge fund accounting can be highly variable from fund to fund and from strategy to strategy.[1] The accounting used for a hedge fund is a by-product of a number of factors, including industry-specific accounting principles and what has been agreed to by a fund's general partner, limited partners, administrator, counsel, and auditor. As it pertains to funds that typically invest directly in small-cap companies—especially in structured financings[2]—there are, nevertheless, some recurring high-level themes that, if better understood by small-cap officers and directors, could save valuable time and resources in workout situations.

PAR

When it comes to valuing convertible instruments—easily the largest source of small-cap workouts—it's common for many hedge funds to initially hold these instruments on their books at par. If the conversion feature of the instrument is "in the money" (the stock is trading at a price that is above the instrument's conversion price), then the convertible instrument might be valued at a premium to par, while if a conversion feature is "under water" (the stock is trading at a price that is below the instrument's conversion price) the convertible instrument might revert to the par valuation. If fund managers decide that a company has underlying operational or fiscal challenges that cast doubt on the par valuation, then funds might seek to discount the par value of (or "impair") a convertible instrument.

The **key point** here is that just because a conversion price is under water doesn't necessarily mean that a fund's P&L is reflecting a loss. Conversely, even though the company's officers and directors might feel optimistic about the company's future, a hedge fund might have impaired the company's convertible instrument all the way to zero.

RESTRICTED

Common shares that underlie convertible instruments can be either legally or functionally restricted. That is, they are legally restricted if they are not covered by an effective registration statement and they are not eligible for resale under Rule 144; in other words, there isn't a public market for the shares. The shares can be functionally restricted because of illiquidity; if a company's stock doesn't trade sufficient volume for a fund to be able to convert an instrument into common shares and sell them without dramatically impacting the stock price, then they are functionally restricted. In either of these situations, funds might apply a valuation discount to more accurately depict the restriction. The **key point** here is that even if the conversion price is materially "in the money," a fund might not be realizing any or all of that on its P&L if the underlying common stock is restricted or illiquid.

WARRANTS

As discussed in Chapter 2, the valuation ascribed to warrants by hedge funds is highly variable, and it's not something funds are likely to disclose. There are some funds that don't apply any value to warrants at all until they are either exercised or the warrants themselves are sold to a third party. At the other end of the spectrum, there are hedge funds that value warrants immediately at their full Black-Scholes valuation.[3] And there is everything in between.[4] The **key point** here is that if a fund negotiates strenuously with respect to warrant coverage, exercise price, and the length of term, then that fund might well value warrants materially on its P&L. Consequently, officers and directors need to consciously take this into account when thinking through how proposals involving warrants might impact the fund's P&L.

TACKING

Although technically not an accounting issue per se, the ability of investors to maintain the benefit of their Rule 144 holding periods, also known as *tacking*, can be an important factor in workouts because it can mean the difference between funds being able to sell common shares (not otherwise registered) or not. The **key point** here is that prior to making any workout proposals to hedge funds, small-cap companies need to check with counsel about how the proposal might impact tacking.

COMMON WORKOUT SCENARIOS

While certainly not intended to be an all-inclusive list, the following are some examples of common workout situations. Each situation highlights how hedge fund psychology and accounting often influence hedge funds to have a completely different perspective from small-cap companies about exactly the same fact pattern.

PENALTIES (LIQUIDATED DAMAGES)

- *Situation*. Small-cap officers and directors often take the position that if they are sufficiently earnest in their request for hedge funds to waive contractual penalties, they will succeed. But from the hedge fund's vantage point, penalties exist for business reasons—to compensate funds for breaches of material terms in definitive financing documents. Therefore, companies can certainly try to extract penalty waivers, but they definitely shouldn't count on them.

- *Different approach*. Rather than repeatedly requesting penalty waivers (which can burn goodwill quickly), officers and directors should think about ways in which they can offer equivalent value without utilizing all-important cash. For example, the company might consider offering to reissue the convertible instrument with a higher principal amount (raised to equal the outstanding penalties) owed the investors at the end of the term. Depending upon the particular fund's accounting approach, this might elevate the par value of the instrument and thus provide a P&L impact similar to cash.[5]

WARRANTS

- *Situation*. Small-cap companies often offer hedge funds the ability to exercise already in-the-money warrants at a lower exercise price in order to offset other loss of value, penalties, or simply as a means of inducing cash exercises. The companies then get frustrated when portfolio managers have no interest in doing that. Companies wonder why anyone in their right mind would turn down free cash.

- *Different Approach*. If an investor doesn't find an offer to exercise "in the money" warrants at a lower exercise price compelling, it's likely because the spread between the stock price and the lowered exercise price is actually less than the Black-Scholes infused value of retaining the warrants on the fund's P&L.[6] In other words, companies have to think through the math before offering to reprice warrants; if the warrants have a long term remaining and the company's stock is highly volatile, then the warrants are likely very valuable.

ANTIDILUTION

- *Situation*: Small-cap companies often have two challenges when they're trying to work out the triggering of an antidilution mechanism in a convertible instrument or warrant. First, companies ask the hedge fund to waive the antidilution adjustment because it's going to make any subsequent financing very challenging (i.e., the new investors don't want all the existing investors to have their conversion or exercise prices lowered). The problem is that waivers of antidilution are almost always sought for the same scenario investors use antidilution provisions in the first place;

existing investors don't want new investors to have the benefit of lower-priced exits. Second, when hedge funds forgo an antidilution adjustment, they are not only potentially failing to capture the spread over the longer term, but they also might be failing to capture a positive P&L impact in the near term.

- *Different approach.* Prior to approaching hedge funds with an antidilution waiver, officers and directors should think through the likely long- and short-term opportunity cost of what the hedge funds are being asked to give up and then suggest some alternative consideration. For example, if the antidilution provision is in the convertible instrument, perhaps the company can consider offering to prepay interest or dividends or increase the amount due the investors at term to offset the lost intrinsic value resulting from the waiver of a lower conversion price. Or if the antidilution provision is in the warrant, perhaps the company could consider increasing the duration of the warrant in order to compensate investors for the opportunity cost of the lost intrinsic value.

DEFAULT

- *Situation.* A common scenario in the small-cap realm is that a convertible note is in default at maturity (i.e., the company is literally out of money), and the company finds a third-party investor to provide some capital to keep the company afloat. But, the third party has two caveats: (1) the company can't use any of the new money to pay off the note in default; and (2) the investor will provide the new capital only if it can replace the existing note holder as a senior secured lender (i.e., the existing note holders need to convert the entire note into common stock). The company approaches the note holder feeling as though it has a fair compromise: the note holders avoid losing all their money and have a chance to be made whole and perhaps even have upside with their common stock in the newly funded company.

- *Different approach*. What small-cap officers and directors routinely neglect to take into consideration in these situations is that the note holders could well have impaired their note all the way to zero already since they were in a position to know that the company wasn't going to be able to pay off the note. Therefore, in such a situation, the note holders have already taken their "medicine" on the fund's P&L, and if they could recover $1,000 in bankruptcy net of expenses, then it could well be financially better for the note holders to go that route instead of surrendering their seniority for common stock in a decidedly risky company. Therefore, rather than assume it wouldn't make any sense for a note holder in this circumstance to force the company into bankruptcy, the officers and directors should consider making an objective decision (perhaps with the help of a third-party expert) to evaluate what the note holders could receive in bankruptcy and consider making a comparable cash offer (by whatever means possible) in lieu of presenting the new investor's demand as a "take it or leave it" situation.

INTEREST OR DIVIDEND PAYMENTS

- *Situation*: Definitive financing documents often set forth explicit situations in which companies are able to pay interest or dividends in stock instead of cash. Typically, these requirements include but are not limited to an effective registration statement covering the common shares; the hedge fund not being in possession of any material, nonpublic information; and the stock trading a predetermined amount of daily dollar volume. When small-cap companies have insufficient cash to pay interest or dividends and the conditions are not met to pay the dividends in stock, companies seek waivers from hedge funds.

- *Different approach*. From the hedge fund's standpoint, the conditions set forth in the deal documents are there for a reason; interest and dividend payments are intended to be in cash. If they aren't, they need to be paid in something that is essentially just as good as cash. In other words, getting lots of common shares in a company with inactively traded stock is not just as good as cash. Therefore, rather than requesting a waiver, because "it's a good thing for the shareholders if the company conserves its cash," companies should consider offering alternative value to investors to offset the lack of cash. For example, the company could consider reissuing the convertible instrument to increase the principal due at term by the amount of the interest or dividend shortfall, especially if the company envisions a continuing inability to pay the interest of dividends in cash going forward. Or the company could consider: amending the instrument to add a make-whole provision; and/or issue the hedge fund some warrants to offset the difference.

CONCLUSION

To be clear, officers and directors should, of course, try to achieve the best results possible for shareholders in any type of workout situation. The intent of proffering these different approaches isn't to suggest that these should be the first things companies offer or that they should necessarily be offered at all. Rather, the goal here is simply to make sure that officers and directors are cognizant of how hedge funds might view these common workout situations so that board room dialogue in this regard can benefit from those sensitivities.

Notes

1. For example, funds that predominantly invest in restricted or highly illiquid securities have unique challenges in valuing those instruments because they often can't realistically sell any or all their stock at market prices, whereas funds that principally invest in large-cap stocks have no such valuation challenges (i.e., the market price is what they could receive for most or all of their position).

2. Structured financings typically create the types of situations that give rise to the most workouts because of their complexity and the array of affirmative and negative covenants.

3. While the Black-Scholes input for time and intrinsic value is self-explanatory, the volatility input used by funds can be variable from one fund to another because the "correct" volatility input is subject to debate.

4. There are some hedge funds that don't value warrants until the common stock underlying the warrants is either registered for resale or salable under Rule 144. Other hedge funds value warrants at a predetermined discount to Black-Scholes.

5. Sometimes companies that have penalties payable to hedge funds offer to issue an equal amount of common stock in lieu of cash. The problem with this approach from a fund's accounting standpoint could be that it mightn't be an equal exchange if, for example, the stock is either restricted or highly illiquid.

6. For example, the hedge fund might capture 25 cents per share with the lowered exercise price (assuming the shares aren't restricted or illiquid), but the warrants themselves might have a Black-Scholes value of 75 cents each if they were sold to a third party.

CHAPTER 8

IPOS AND INDEPENDENT DIRECTORS

IPOs and IPO Alternatives

Key considerations for independent directors:

- It's easy to lose sight of the fact that directors represent all shareholders, not just the large shareholders.
- Are the directors being brutally realistic about whether the company is ready to be public?
- IPO success stories abound, but the board also needs to focus on worst-case scenarios. It's critical to be students of recent history, especially with IPO alternatives.

Common mistakes to avoid:

- Being unduly influenced by large shareholders.
- Materially underestimating the distraction and expense of going public and being public.
- Having inadequate backup plans if the IPO is delayed or withdrawn.
- Failing to appreciate the hidden costs to shareholders of IPO alternatives.

Although this book is principally about the unique challenges faced by small-cap directors, it's worth delving briefly into some of the underappreciated governance issues faced by independent directors during the time that precedes the IPO process, since these issues are recurring themes in most small-cap boardrooms where financing is being analyzed.

FIDUCIARY OBLIGATIONS TO ALL SHAREHOLDERS

Very few directors are incapable of reciting the legal axiom that directors owe their fiduciary obligations to the corporation and its shareholders. This straightforward principle consistently gets bastardized when directors are, in effect, appointed to boards by large or controlling investors. In the context of pre-IPO companies, private equity and venture capital firms typically have someone from their firm or a designee on the board of directors. And, in companies that are already public, it's not uncommon for large investors to seek to have board designees as well. In each of these situations, of course, the director doesn't represent the interests of management or the investment firm. Rather the director represents the corporation itself and all shareholders. In practice, however, conflicts of interest abound.

Consider the pre-IPO context more specifically, where boards not only contain directors from private equity or venture capital firms or their designees, but also might even have contractual rights to a majority of board seats at certain times. In the best-case scenario, all independent directors undertake their fiduciary obligations as required under applicable laws. In the worst-case scenario, however, independent directors are unduly influenced by the interests of the largest shareholders to the detriment of minority shareholders and the company. To better understand how a conflict of interest might evolve, consider the following example.

Company ABC has two large institutional investors whose designees occupy four of the seven seats on ABC's board. While ABC is performing well, it still doesn't have demonstrable visibility with respect to its revenue and margins, it has two customers that account for 80 percent of its revenue, and it lacks sophisticated internal financial controls or reporting infrastructure. ABC's two large investors are attempting to raise money for new investment funds, and it would be helpful to their fundraising if they were able to show prospective investors that their portfolio companies frequently have liquidity events (i.e., IPOs). In assessing whether ABC should attempt to undertake an IPO, the four designee board members have, in some sense, fairly simple choices to make—they are going to objectively weigh the pros and cons of whether ABC is a good IPO candidate and is ready to be a public company, or they are going to do what's best for the two largest shareholders. To be sure, sometimes what is best for the largest shareholders is best for all the shareholders. And sometimes it isn't.

For better or worse, this scenario unfolds repeatedly every year, in part, because IPOs are an industry unto themselves and are highly influenced by institutional investors. For example, from 2007 through 2011, there were 587 IPOs that raised approximately $170 billion.[1] And of the approximately $170 billion raised, private equity and venture capital-backed deals accounted for approximately 44 percent of that total.[2] Many of the companies that register for IPOs each year are ready to be public companies, and the decision to be public is in all the shareholders' best interests. But, there are also many companies that waste inordinate amounts of time, effort, money, and opportunity unsuccessfully trying to go public, in part, because directors are unduly influenced by large investors. There is an undeniable bias in favor of becoming a public company in the United States, and there is more than enough systemic financial incentive to impact the propriety of governance decision making.

The **key point** here is that in pre-IPO situations (and again once public), independent board members have to focus on the interests of *all* shareholders *all* the time.

TIP

When evaluating joining the board of a pre-IPO company where there are large institutional investors with board representation, prospective independent directors should, among other things, consider: (1) whether and to what extent large investors seek to influence board conduct exclusively in their favor; (2) whether and to what extent existing board members attempt to be objective in their decision making as opposed to treating different shareholders differently; and (3) whether and to what extent the large investors' other portfolio companies appear to have rigorous, independent corporate governance.

ARE DIRECTORS BEING REALISTIC OR OPTIMISTIC ABOUT AN IPO?

There are countless books, seminars, and professional practice guides from law firms, investment banks, and consulting firms that set forth in granular detail how a board should analyze whether a private company is ready to be a public company. Although sometimes helpful, much of this literature suffers from two conspicuous shortcomings: (1) it's typically not written by those who actually have first-hand experience making governance decisions; and (2) it's largely created and circulated by entities that profit from IPOs. Therefore, many pre-IPO boards are left with little objective, practical guidance when it matters most—during the early, formative, consensus-building discussions about whether going public is realistic and a good thing for all the shareholders.

In order to skew board dialogue in this regard from subjective to objective, from optimistic to realistic, and to thwart partisan influence in the boardroom, following are seven issues for directors to analyze:

1. *Recent industry comparables.* It's instructive for any board considering an IPO to start by examining other companies in the same industry that have transacted IPOs in the previous 12 to 18 months. How does the company's size and financial performance compare to those that have recently gone public? How have those other companies performed in the market after their listings? If no other companies in the same industry have gone public in the previous 12 to 18 months, why? Are there companies in the industry that have filed for IPOs but have still not transacted their offerings? If so, how does the company's size and financial performance compare to them?

2. *Overall industry comparables.* How does the company's size and financial performance compare to all the publicly traded companies in the same industry (i.e., not just the companies that have recently gone public)?

3. *Industry IPO pipeline.* If other companies in the industry pipeline have already filed to go public, how does the company's size and financial performance compare to them? Is there anything positive or negative about going public after those companies (are any of those other companies tough acts to follow)? If there isn't a pipeline of other companies in the industry, why not?

4. *Timing.* Is the company sufficiently mature that it can continue on its current growth trajectory even with the material expense and distraction of an IPO? Will it be particularly impactful on the company's competitiveness when its financial statements are made public? How have all the publicly traded companies in the industry been performing?

5. *Expenses.* Service providers will provide clients with varying estimates about the expenses associated with going public.

But the board needn't rely on this information exclusively; rather the board should analyze the securities filings of other companies in the industry that have recently gone public to see how much it cost them. Moreover, the expenses of going public are only part of the overall expense equation, inasmuch as operating expenditures can increase dramatically for public companies. The board should analyze the securities filings of publicly traded industry competitors to quantify differences between operating expenses on a line item basis and as a percentage of net revenue. Has the company adequately factored these expenses into its operating models?

6. *Internal controls.* Regardless of the legislative and regulatory compliance mandates applicable to a particular company at the time of its IPO, the board should assume that investor expectations with respect to public companies are the same whether a company has been public for 30 days or 30 years. Therefore, boards need to be especially cognizant of whether the company's financial reporting and operational controls are sufficiently thorough and sophisticated to withstand public scrutiny. Prior to undertaking the time and expense of a compliance/controls audit from a third party, the board should consider inviting a seasoned public company audit chairperson to provide a compliance/controls overview against which the company can compare itself.

7. *Management.* The board should carefully compare and contrast the company's management with the qualifications and credibility of officers of publicly traded competitors. Toward this end, the board should even consider attending investor conferences where publicly traded competitors are presenting their companies in order to get a better sense of them. Although this is admittedly not an objective exercise like the others,

it's no less critical because the skill set required to excel as public company management can be quite different from the skills required for successful private company leadership.

The **key point** here is that the likeliest point of failure in an ill-advised IPO isn't in the selection of bankers, the S-1 filing, or the road-show. Rather it's during the determinative early board discussions about the relative merits of pursuing an IPO where conscientious realism can easily be replaced by optimistic tunnel vision.

> TIP
>
> Although it happens repeatedly, there is no excuse for a board's failure to appreciate the added expenses associated with undertaking an IPO and being a public company. In Ernst & Young LLPs, "True Costs of IPOs Survey," (2011), that firm examined 26 companies that went public in the United States between 2009 and 2011. The results showed that, on average, the companies surveyed (which had median annual revenues of $143 million) spent $13 million in one-time advisory costs in connection with the IPO (e.g., bankers, lawyers, auditors, financial printer, stock transfer agent, Sarbanes-Oxley consultant, etc.), and they spent an average of $2.5 million annually post-IPO in extra operating expenses ($1.5 million of which was added management and governance compensation to attract and retain top talent).

WORST-CASE SCENARIOS

Regardless of what type of financing is being discussed in most pre-IPO or small-cap boardrooms, directors need to focus on worst-case scenarios because enterprise risk is often austere in the absence of growth capital. That is, what if the company doesn't complete the financing within a certain time frame? What if the company doesn't complete the financing at all? Or what if the financing is transacted but for less money than the company required? Although there are fantastic success stories, IPOs can also have less than successful results.

More specifically, in 2010 and 2011, there were 520 companies that made filings with the SEC to go public.[3] But during the same period, there were only 279 companies that went public.[4] In other words, during the period 47 percent of the filing companies did not transact an IPO. This two-year period may not be a historically representative sample of the percentage of successes relating to going public. However, boards need to be prepared for IPOs to be delayed or withdrawn—it's a very real prospect.

To complicate matters for pre-IPO boards, the delay or withdrawal of an IPO can result in more than just lost capital. It can also result in:

1. *Stigma.* For better or worse, the delay or withdrawal of an IPO carries with it the image of failure both inside and outside the company, and this image could affect the company's ability to: garner alternative financing; retain employees; maintain the same relationships with suppliers; and compete in the marketplace.

2. *Disclosure.*[5] Once a company files its Form S-1 registration statement with the SEC in order to go public, the company is not able to thoroughly retract that information (i.e., even if the S-1 is subsequently withdrawn the information has likely been parsed by many interested parties). Consequently, employees, suppliers, and competitors are not only privy to detailed financial information about the company, but they might attempt to use that information to the detriment of the company.

3. *Biting the hand that feeds.* Often, the most realistic source of alternate funding should an IPO fail to materialize is large existing investors, but conflicts of interest can develop within a board, and this can jeopardize that funding. For example, when a board is divided about whether or not

to withdraw an IPO (i.e., the large investors are in favor of proceeding with the IPO, but the board in inclined to withdrawal), a decision to withdraw might jeopardize alternative financing.

The **key point** here is that given the meaningful percentage of filing companies that have failed to transact IPOs combined with the possibly penal consequences of a delay or withdrawal, directors of pre-IPO companies would be best served by working toward the best outcome (i.e., a successful IPO) but planning diligently for the worst.

TIP

It's challenging for directors to adequately prepare for the likely headwinds caused by a withdrawn IPO if they've never had that experience. Therefore, directors are well advised to seek out other directors who've been through the process and learn as much as possible from them about what to expect. The best source of referrals is bankers, lawyers, and auditors, all of whom have just as much experience with withdrawn IPOs as completed IPOs.

IPO ALTERNATIVES

Although rarely considered by private equity and venture capital-backed private companies, there are a several ways for a private company to become a publicly traded company other than the standard, firmly underwritten IPO which boards may well consider:

1. *Reverse merger.* Private companies can substantially obviate the time and expense of a traditional IPO by merging with an existing public company, whereby the private company ends up being the controlling or surviving entity.[6] Typically in a reverse

merger private companies merge into a shell company; that is, a fully reporting, publicly traded company that for various reasons no longer has any business operations. Alternatively, a private company can reverse into its own freshly created shell that begins reporting to the SEC (by filing a Form 10), and thereafter applies to an exchange to have its shares publicly traded. In either of these instances, a financing can be undertaken simultaneously with or subsequent to the mergers.

2. *SPAC.* A special purpose acquisition company, (SPAC) is a public shell company that is formed for the purpose of acquiring a company. It raises proceeds in its own IPO, and those proceeds are held in trust. The SPAC must sign a letter of intent to acquire a company typically within 12 to 18 months of the IPO (and this acquisition must be approved by the shareholders), or the SPAC's capital is returned to the shareholders. Any company that is acquired by a SPAC would then effectively be publicly traded.

Primary Consideration for Directors—History

The alternatives to IPOs are typically faster and cheaper than traditional IPOs, and some have been successful (e.g., the NYSE went public via a reverse merger). But directors who are considering these alternatives need to be mindful of the fact that for better or worse investors are still largely predisposed to companies that become public through traditional means for several reasons: (1) especially in the case of reverse mergers into trading shells[7] and SPACs, the filings and disclosures are far less rigorous than the typical regulatory filings associated with an IPO; (2) these alternative routes to the public markets aren't typically accompanied by the stamps of approval from well-known auditing and investment banking firms; (3) particularly in the case of reverse mergers into trading shells, there are often preexisting contingent liabilities from the company's prior operating life that can come back to haunt the merged entity; (4) in the case of reverse mergers into trading shells and SPACs, there are preexisting investors who own freely tradable shares whose intentions can be challenging to assess; and (5) particularly in the case of reverse mergers into trading shells, most of those companies don't trade on senior U.S. exchanges.[8]

The **key point** here is that with all the data now available,[9] directors can streamline their analyses of issues like these by focusing on historical facts. For example, when was the last time that a company in the same industry undertook one of these alternate paths, and how has that company performed as a public company?[10] If there aren't any recent industry comparables, then directors should examine the last half-dozen similar sized companies that pursued one of these alternatives and analyze how those companies have performed as public companies. Last, but certainly not least, directors who are analyzing the merits of an alternative IPO as opposed to staying private need to be mindful that just because it's cheaper and faster than a traditional IPO doesn't mean that it's cheap and fast. Therefore, when comparable companies that have transacted an alternative IPO are identified, it's a good idea to try to understand from their experiences a little bit more about the timeline and expense of the process since there is far less reliable data in that regard than there is about traditional IPOs.

TIP

For directors who are considering a reverse merger, here are some statistics from DealFlow Media: (1) through the first three quarters of 2010 there was a total of $279 million invested in reverse merged entities, and through the first three quarters of 2011 there was a total of $82 million invested; and (2) in 2008 the total combined market capitalization of all reverse merged entities was over $3 billion, and in 2012 the total combined market capitalization of all reverse merged entities was approximately $400 million. While these statistics alone shouldn't dictate a board's decision making process, it is nevertheless important to take note of the hidden costs for shareholders; that is, for shareholders to ultimately benefit from an alternative IPO (vs. remaining private), there needs to be capital available to finance the business once it's public, and there needs to be a sufficiently vibrant market for the stocks.

For directors who are considering SPACs, the marketplace is small; that is, as of April 2012, according to DealFlow Media, there were 22 trading SPACs, and the majority of them had a prescribed industry mandate. For example, if a private semiconductor company were seeking a SPAC, only 9 of the 22 could consider it based on their investing verticals.

Notes

1. *Global IPO Review 2011*, http://www.renaissancecapital.com, 3 (U.S. statistics include IPOs with a market cap of at least $50 million and exclude closed-end funds and SPACs).

2. Ibid. (based on statistics therein).

3. Ibid., 7.

4. Ibid., 3.

5. The JOBS Act contains a provision that allows "emerging growth companies," as that term is defined in the act, to file registration statements confidentially. Thereafter, registration statements need to be made available to the public a minimum of 21 days prior to a company commencing its IPO roadshow. Time will tell how this provision is utilized by companies, but it certainly minimizes the risk of disclosure without a corresponding IPO.

6. For a detailed discussion of structural, procedural, and legal issues surrounding IPO alternatives see, Steven Dresner, *The Issuer's Guide to PIPEs* (New York: Bloomberg Press, 2009), 283–335, and David N. Feldman, *Reverse Mergers: And Other Alternatives to Traditional IPOs* (New York: Bloomberg Financial, 2009).

7. In June 2011, the SEC went so far as to issue an investor bulletin regarding reverse mergers in which it warns prospective investors that, "Many companies either fail or struggle to remain viable after completing a reverse merger." SEC Office of Investor Education and Advocacy, "*Investor Bulletin: Reverse Mergers,*" http://www. sec.gov/investor/alerts/reversemergers.pdf, 2.

8. As is discussed later in the book in more detail, when a company's stock doesn't trade on a senior exchange (i.e., NYSE, or Nasdaq), there are often material

consequences for shareholders; such as fewer market makers, higher bid/ask spreads, more volatility, less volume, less or no equity research, penny stock restrictions, and the inability for many institutional investors to own the stock.

9. Services like PrivateRaise, Dealogic, Knobias, Capital IQ, and Placement-Tracker offer the ability to track enormous amounts of small-cap financing data.

10. When reviewing how a particular company has performed as a public company after an alternative public offering, it's important for directors to not only look at the stock price and market price, but also at the daily volume of shares traded, the exchange its traded on, and the audited financials. A company might well have a compelling stock price and market capitalization, but if it's very thinly traded resulting from, among other things, a controlled float, and it's also not traded on a senior exchange, then the stock price and market capitalization could well be misleading. Moreover, it's important for directors to analyze the quality of the audited financials, particularly if the auditing firm is not well-recognized.

PART 2

CAPITAL MARKETS

W hile a stock's price and the manner in which it trades are important to public companies of all sizes, these matters take on an altogether different poignancy for small-cap companies—they're often a matter of life and death.

A small-cap company can dutifully follow every nuance set forth in Part One and still end up with an egregiously dilutive financing or no capital all, if it has a *bad* stock. As discussed in the introduction to Part One, it is a uniquely small-cap phenomenon that there are comparatively well-run companies that have *bad* stocks, and there are less compelling companies that have *good* stocks.[1] It goes without saying that having a *good* stock is preferable (and being a high-quality company with a *good* stock is, of course, the goal); having a *good* stock makes it considerably easier for small-cap companies to raise capital, makes it considerably cheaper to raise capital, and makes it more attractive for investors to buy the stock in the open market.

A GOOD STOCK

Operating quality of the company notwithstanding, there are five components of a *good* small-cap stock:

1. *Trading volume.* Trading volume is the most important component for any small-cap stock. If individual investors or institutions can't buy or sell stocks in meaningful amounts without the stock skyrocketing or plummeting, then they simply won't buy them in the first place. Trading volume makes financings easier and cheaper for high-quality companies, and even the riskiest company can get financing if its stock trades in sufficient volume. Ample trading volume is not only a corporate finance elixir for small-cap stocks, but for companies that are performing well, it's also a prerequisite for equity research coverage and institutional sponsorship.

2. *Price.* Like larger public companies, it's always beneficial when a small-cap company's stock trades at a premium compared to peer valuations. But, the actual stock price is a critical component for small-cap companies because there are some institutions, for example, that can't buy stocks that are priced under $5, and there are still other institutions that won't own stocks with a price in the single digits.

3. *Equity research coverage.* Equity research coverage is a critical component for small-cap stocks, because: (a) it represents third-party diligence and validation; (b) it gets corporate financial models about otherwise unknown companies into the hands of investors; and (c) companies can leverage institutional sales personnel from investment banks (the "sell-side") to help market the company's stock.

4. *Stability*. Small-cap stocks are often considerably more volatile than are larger public company stocks because of the inherently less predictable nature of smaller companies, the corresponding susceptibility to market innuendo, and lower trading volumes. Small-cap stocks that are more stable than peer companies have an advantage because volatile price swings can scare away prospective investors.

5. *Minimal short interest*. The extent to which investors bet against a stock's price appreciation by effectuating short sales is a polarizing discussion topic in many small-cap boardrooms resulting in large measure from speculation and misinformation. Although there are certainly instances in the small-cap universe where stocks develop a high short interest (i.e., the proportion of investors betting against a stock's price appreciation is disproportionate when compared to peers) for reasons having little to do with company fundamentals, more often than not a high short interest is the result of poor communication, controversial management, skepticism about operational performance, or doubts about financial reporting. Even if the merits of the short "case" are questionable, a high short interest can in and of itself make financings more expensive and deter prospective investors. Therefore, minimal short interest, if any, is preferable to the alternative.

WHY BAD STOCKS HAPPEN TO GOOD COMPANIES

While it's entirely understandable and intuitive why operationally challenged companies would have correspondingly illiquid, ignored, and undervalued stocks, it's often more vexing for small-cap directors to understand why an otherwise well-performing company could endure a similar fate. It's often a combination of four actions and omissions that causes this to happen:

1. *Flawed Street communication.* Especially since many small-cap management teams are inexperienced in operating public companies, problems communicating with the Street are ubiquitous. Communications problems range from chronically overpromising and underdelivering and serially issuing immaterial press releases, to combative investor meetings and inconsistent messaging. These actions can result in a depressed stock price, greater volatility, and an elevated short interest.

2. *Lack of Street communication.* Another reason bad stocks happen to good small-cap companies is when management and directors reach the conclusion that they are going to "focus on just executing on the business, and the rest will take care of itself." Unless a company is experiencing dramatic year-over-year growth in a sector that's in favor, typically this omission can result in low trading volume, a depressed stock price, and lack of interest from equity research analysts.

3. *Sell-side vacuum.* Many small-cap officers and directors don't sufficiently understand the sell-side business model and how equity research analysts make money. Therefore, there is often a disjointed or nonexistent effort to court appropriately situated equity research analysts. In addition to this omission, there are also legions of small-cap companies that are too small or have stocks that are too inactively traded for equity research analysts to even consider. No matter what the cause, the lack of equity research coverage can result in a depressed stock price, greater volatility, and lower trading volume.

4. *Efforts to boost stock price.* Small-cap officers and directors are often besieged with advice from hedge funds about measures

that could boost a company's stock price in the near term, including but not limited to stock buy-backs, dividends, and reverse stock splits. Unfortunately, these actions sometimes have unintended consequences when undertaken by many small-cap companies such as share price erosion, lower trading volume, elevated short interest, alienated equity research analysts, and greater volatility.

GOVERNANCE ISSUE

Overseeing the development of an effective capital markets strategy and its execution are board responsibilities at the vast majority of small-cap companies, because the absence of this can cause crippling enterprise risk.

Notwithstanding the fact that having a bad stock can augment a small-cap company's cost of, or even access to, capital, there are many small-cap directors who still fail to adequately appreciate the myriad risks created by an ineffective capital markets strategy and the errors and omissions that exacerbate the problem.

Therefore, the purpose of Part Two is to provide directors with a better understanding of capital markets issues that are critical to the success of any small-cap company and also provide directors with a methodology for analyzing some of the capital markets situations that are regularly faced.

CHAPTER 9

TRADING VOLUME IS EVERYTHING

Volume, Volume, Volume

Key considerations for directors:

- The more trading volume a small-cap company's stock has, the more alternatives the company has.
- Trading volume makes equity financings cheaper and easier.
- Trading volume facilitates institutional ownership and equity research coverage.
- Retail investors—not institutional investors—initially supply trading volume to small-cap stocks.
- Institutional investors are easier to target/identify than retail investors, but math principally determines whether institutional investors can own a given small-cap stock.

Common mistakes to avoid:

- Small-cap directors routinely fail to appreciate the importance of trading volume.
- Many small-cap officers and directors lack any cohesive plan to build ample and sustainable trading volume.
- Small-cap companies waste excessive amounts of time and money speaking with investors who can't buy the company's stock.
- There are no shortcuts to building sustainable trading volume.

I f location, location, and location are the three things that matter most to retail stores, then volume, volume, and volume are the three things that matter most to most small-cap stocks.

The more trading volume a small-cap stock has, the easier it is to undertake equity financings and the cheaper the cost of that capital for a relatively simple reason. The faster and easier it is for investors to sell a position, the less concerned they are about disastrous downside scenarios, and the more easily they can opportunistically take advantage of price appreciation. Put a different way, if investors can't get out in good times or bad times, they're either not going to get in to begin with or they are going to a charge a premium to offset the risk of illiquidity.

The more trading volume a small-cap stock has, the easier it is for investors to accumulate meaningful positions in the open market. And investors who accumulate meaningful positions are more likely to buy stocks that are actively traded because the prices don't skyrocket and plummet when comparatively small amounts of stock are bought and sold. For example, if an investor is trying to buy 10,000 shares of a stock, and this purchase pushes the price up by 15 percent, the investor is simply going to choose another stock.

The more trading volume a small-cap stock has, the more likely it is to attract equity research analysts, who, in turn, can assist with marketing the stock to institutional investors. In other words, if a stock doesn't trade in sufficient volume for an equity research analyst's clients to buy it, then the equity research analyst isn't going to make any money covering the stock.

The more trading volume a small-cap stock has, the more likely it can use that stock as a currency to buy other companies. For example, why would another company accept an all stock acquisition offer if the stock doesn't trade in sufficient volume for the acquisition consideration to ever be monetized?

The more trading volume a small-cap stock has, the more value employee retention tools (e.g., stock options) have. For example, employees are not going to stay at the company because of in-the-money stock options, if the company's stock doesn't trade in sufficient volume to enable employees to exercise the options and sell the stock.

In essence, trading volume in small-cap stocks is tantamount to alternatives. Every small-cap capital markets veteran has favorite examples of companies that were able to pursue a half-dozen or more disparate products, services, or business models prior to finding success, and the common characteristic among them is often trading volume. Trading volume facilitates access to the equity capital markets,[2] and, cash provides business options. Hence, a conspicuous lack of trading volume leaves a small-cap company with a dangerously low margin for error.

TIP

Today there is a $50 billion plus annual marketplace where hedge funds invest directly in predominantly small-cap companies. The private investment in public equity (PIPE) industry arose in the 1990s for two principal reasons: (1) the small investment banks that specialized in transacting public offerings for small public companies went through a period of consolidation, leaving legions of small-cap companies with an inability to raise capital; and (2) hedge funds were foreclosed from meaningfully investing in otherwise attractive small public companies because they were too illiquid. The result was symbiotic, inasmuch as small-cap companies were always in need of growth capital, and hedge funds couldn't invest except for the ability to purchase the stock directly from the companies. The **key point** here is that even though the PIPE market came to the fore because of rampant small-cap illiquidity, there is often a demonstrable benefit afforded small-cap companies with active trading volume, especially in the wake of the financial crisis.

Not surprisingly, the question small-cap directors ask most often is, what is an appropriate target liquidity for a company's stock? Although there are no hard and fast rules in this regard, directors should just keep it simple; that is, a small-cap company has ample trading volume if small-cap institutional investors can buy and sell the stock in the ordinary course of business for a price that is at or near the quoted price.[3] But, there is no such thing as a small-cap stock that is *too* liquid.

THE TRADING VOLUME CONUNDRUM

As important as trading volume is to the success of small-cap companies, it's also as widely misunderstood by many small-cap directors as it is elusive. There are a number of reasons why the importance and nuances of trading volume are poorly understood by many small-cap directors:

1. *Capital markets experience.* As set forth in the Introduction, and throughout Part One, most small-cap boards lack directors with material small-cap[4] capital markets experience. Additionally, and as also discussed previously, many small-cap management teams are inexperienced in operating public companies of any size.

2. *Not intuitive.* The most sensible way for the uninitiated to view the ebb and flow of capital in the stock market is to understand that companies that are performing well will attract the most shareholder interest. And that's true, for example, in the Fortune 500, where there are a limited number of companies that are conspicuously well known and meticulously dissected by hordes of professional and amateur analysts, bloggers, and so on. However, that is considerably less true for the thousands of small-cap companies that operate in near obscurity to the extent that even if they were handily outdistancing their peers, hardly anyone might know.

3. *Service providers.* In addition to the lack of capital markets experience among many small-cap officers and directors, the service providers employed by small-cap companies often don't have capital markets experience or don't have a vested interest in focusing on the repercussions of a company's trading volume. More specifically, trading volume is inapplicable to the services provided by attorneys and auditors; small-cap investment bankers often ply their trade with whatever trading volume hand they are dealt and then move on to the next transaction. Many investor relations firms understandably seek to deemphasize trading volume data lest the entire value of their professional services be reduced to a periodic referendum on a single metric that they don't control.

4. *White noise.* Given the sheer number of small-cap companies, attorneys, auditors, bankers, and investor relations professionals, there are so many viewpoints about issues like trading volume that it's challenging for small-cap directors to separate the wheat from the chaff.

In addition to being misunderstood, trading volume is also elusive for many small-cap companies. For example, as set forth in Figure 9.1, a Nasdaq company with a $100 million market capitalization has a median average daily trading volume (ADTV) of approximately 0.25 percent of its issued and outstanding shares. In other words, if a $100 million company has 50 million shares issued and outstanding and trades for $2.00, its median ADTV would be approximately 125,000 shares per day (or approximately $250,000). Since that number isn't terribly helpful in a vacuum, the following statistics provide some instructive context:

- The median institutional ownership of a $100 million Nasdaq company is only 37 percent.

- The average $100 million Nasdaq company has only one research analyst, and one out of every four companies that size has no research coverage at all.

- Almost one in three $100 million Nasdaq companies doesn't even trade half as much volume as the median case in Figure 9.1.[5]

To be clear, median liquidity in larger companies grows considerably. That is, if you were to consider a $500 million Nasdaq company that has 100 million shares issued and outstanding and trades for $5.00, its median ADTV would be approximately 650,000 shares per day (or approximately $3,250,000). In addition:

- The median institutional ownership of a $500 million Nasdaq company is 81 percent.

- The average $500 million Nasdaq company has six research analysts, and only 4 percent of companies that size have no research coverage at all.

- Fewer than two in ten $500 million Nasdaq companies have lower ADTV's than the median case.[6]

While liquidity for companies that are $500 million and larger is considerable, it's important to be mindful that (as discussed in the Introduction) seven out of every ten public companies in the United States

Figure 9-1: **Nasdaq Trading Volumes**

Market cap range (Millions)	Median market cap (Millions)	Median ADTV[7]
$0–$41	$21	0.17%
$41–$119	$72	0.25%
$119–$301	$189	0.40%
$301–$926	$526	0.65%

Source: Keating Investments, LLC

have *less* than a $500 million market capitalization. For those companies trading volume is often an austere struggle. Given this conundrum of misinformation and elusiveness, what's most important for small-cap directors to understand is how boards can strategically assist management in their efforts to generate more trading volume and at the same time better understand why some actions or omissions in this regard can have unintended consequences.

HOW SUSTAINABLE TRADING VOLUME IS GENERATED

There is, perhaps, no other issue that vexes more small-cap directors than why two companies that might appear quite similar to a third party could have stocks that trade appreciably different volumes. At the root of this issue is often a fundamental lack of understanding of how sustainable trading volume is generated. Like constructing anything else that is durable and sustainable, generating trading volume is a process based on certain axioms, and no matter what anyone might argue to the contrary, there are no short cuts.[8]

CORPORATE EXECUTION

Nearly every small-cap director knows that the basis for generating long-biased[9] investor interest (i.e., investors who believe the stock's value will rise, as opposed to short-biased investors who believe the stock's value will fall) is reliable, compelling financial performance that distinguishes a company from its peers. But where many small-cap directors go astray is in their presupposition that financial performance is not only the basis of generating trading volume, but it's the only catalyst. Unlike large public companies in which positively differentiated financial results are immediately parsed, digested, and acted upon resulting from ubiquitous information, many small-cap companies have to first create the audience.

TIP

As alluded to in Part One, Chapter 1, there is an exception to the rule that corporate execution is the exclusive basis for sustainable trading volume and the exception is a uniquely small-cap phenomenon. More specifically, there are myriad examples of extensive trading volume in small-cap stocks where such trading volume has little if anything to do with the comparative financial performance of the operating company. Rather, the trading becomes almost unhinged from the underlying operating company, and traders with all different types of motivations trade in and out of the stock. Sometimes this is inspired by controversy as opposed to valuation, sometimes it's a result of a charismatic or promotional CEO, sometimes it is inspired by prior performance, and sometimes it is sector driven. But, regardless of the reason, the **key point** here for small-cap directors is clear; sometimes constructively reaching out to an apt audience with a *good* message pays more dividends in the small-cap ecosystem than delivering a *great* message to the wrong audience or being *best in class* but not communicating at all.

Who Is the Audience?

The audience for many small-cap stocks isn't dictated by qualitative measures nearly as much as it is by math. That is, if a stock is too illiquid for institutional investors to buy in the ordinary course of their business without pushing the stock price up appreciably, then the proper audience for the stock isn't institutional investors. Easily one of the most underappreciated facts among small-cap officers and directors is that developing trading volume that is sufficient to facilitate institutional trading is generated first from retail investors. Retail investors (i.e., individual investors and/or nonprofessional investors) typically purchase considerably smaller positions than do institutional investors, and they are also less sensitive to the purchase price. Therefore, it is retail investors who supply all the volume in the capital markets for small-cap companies until such time as the trading volume is material enough to support institutional investors.[10]

TIP

A very helpful, free tool that is vastly underutilized by small-cap officers and directors is reviewing the institutional holdings "tab" at nasdaq.com for the company as well as for peer companies. Upon review of the various institutional holdings, it will become quite clear whether and to what extent institutions are interested in *and able to* buy these related stocks.

EFFECTIVELY REACHING RETAIL INVESTORS

When small-cap officers and directors realize that they need to predominantly market the company's stock to retail investors in order to generate sufficient trading volume for institutional investors, it's an important step; but, it's also the easy part. The challenging part is constructively reaching interested, receptive retail investors considering that it's a notoriously challenging, fragmented market. When it comes to reaching retail investors, there isn't really one-stop-shopping. Rather, there are a number of tools at the disposal of small-cap companies that together can form a sensible, effective outreach, and it's important for small-cap directors to understand these tools so that they can ensure that officers are considering them. It's critically important that for each of the various methodologies set forth below board members make sure that management *has first secured relevant references confirming effectiveness and return on investment*, and that, where appropriate, management has also consulted counsel:

• *Investor relations firms.* As is presented with greater specificity in Part Three, investor relations firms are a great starting point and can be of tremendous help if they have a demonstrated track record of reaching retail investors for a company with a substantially similar capital markets profile. As it pertains to retail investor outreach, it's also very possible that a firm that assists the company with retail investors might not necessarily be the best choice for the company once the outreach becomes more institutional.

- *Public relations.* Public relations is often overlooked by small-cap officers and directors primarily because investor relations intuitively seems more targeted to those most likely to buy stock. That may well be the case for institutional outreach, but it's not necessarily true at all when it comes to retail investor outreach. Ongoing, well-placed news stories (either online or in print) in mass media, business publications, trade publications, and/or on television can be tremendously effective in reaching retail investors. Moreover, there is an increasingly important social media subset to traditional public relations that involves cultivating relationships with, for example, influential industry and capital markets bloggers (i.e., mainstream offline media increasingly look to influential online content for story ideas). The **key point** here for small-cap directors to understand is that one story in *USA Today* could actually be more helpful in generating retail investor interest than 25 investor luncheons held around the country.

- *Opt-in stock newsletters.* Small-cap officers and directors should be receptive to considering opt-in stock newsletters (opt-in newsletters are sent to subscribers as opposed to unsolicited stock newsletters) that have compelling references. While such newsletters can certainly contain more hype than substance, there are online and offline newsletters that have dedicated followings of active retail investors who are keen on finding the next "unknown" company. And, ultimately, for many small-cap companies trying to generate more trading volume, a good part of the challenge is simply reaching interested investors with the company's story.

- *Opt-in e-mail/digital outreach*: Just like stock newsletters, the Internet is rife with disingenuous small-cap stock marketing promotions. But there are, nevertheless, Internet-based opt-in marketing opportunities (opt-in Internet-based marketing is sent to subscribers as oppose to unsolicited outreach or "spam") that small-cap officers and directors should be receptive to provided that the references are acceptable.

TIP

When trying to reach retail investors, it's critical that small-cap officers and directors resist throwing the proverbial baby out with the bath water. That is, many officers and directors are too quick to roll their collective eyes when they are approached with an "online marketing program" to assist in raising a company's profile with retail investors. To be sure, healthy skepticism is appropriate. But given how challenging reaching retail investors can be and how critical trading volume is to most small-cap companies, officers and directors need to consider creative outreach approaches that have real references. As an example, there are vendors that enable companies to issue their latest press releases in real time to any investor who just typed in a competitor's ticker symbol at major financial websites. While such outreach doesn't facilitate sustainable trading volume by itself, it can accomplish the important goal of getting the company's name in front of a highly qualified reader/investor. The **key point** here for officers and directors is that just because a lot of small-cap stock marketing on the Internet is disingenuous doesn't mean that the Internet is a poor channel for the company's content.

EFFECTIVELY REACHING INSTITUTIONAL INVESTORS

Just as there are retail investors who might seek to buy $500 of a particular stock, and others who might seek to buy $25,000 of a stock, it often gets overlooked that institutional investors who buy small-cap stocks[11] are similarly varied. That is, small funds might buy only $250,000 positions in a given company, while larger funds might seek positions that are two hundred times that amount.[12] Therefore, most small-cap companies evolve from retail investors to small institutional investors to larger institutional investors. But unlike the fragmentation of retail investors, reaching institutional investors is considerably more targeted, because the universe of small-cap institutional investors is finite, and the investing preferences of most of the active small-cap investors are well known[13]:

TIP

Small-cap officers and directors are often unclear about when the company is really in a position to begin reaching out to institutional investors (in addition to retail investors). Although there aren't any hard and fast rules, some math might help to put the issue into better perspective. Assume for purposes of discussion that the company's stock trades $100,000 per day on average. Although there are exceptions, it can often be challenging to buy more than 10 to 15 percent of the daily volume of some small-cap stocks without pushing up the price of the stock. Therefore, if a fund would like to build a $250,000 position in the company's stock within a certain price range, it could easily take 15 to 20 trading days (i.e., an entire month). And that's assuming that the stock stays flat (or in the desired buy-in range) for the entire month. When you consider the volatility of small-cap companies and the fact that portfolio managers sometimes monitor dozens of positions, quite a few stars have to line up for this fund to establish its starter position in the course of a month. If it were a $1 million starter position, it could easily take three to four months or more in this example. In reality, many small-cap funds won't consider positions that take longer than five to ten trading days to acquire. The **key point** here for officers and directors is that, conventional wisdom notwithstanding, institutional investors can't simply press a few buttons and own many small-cap stocks in a day or so like is possible with large-cap stocks. The longer it takes to acquire a position, the less likely funds will consider it. Plus if it takes that long to buy, it could take even longer to sell.

- *Investor relations/direct.* As is the case with reaching out to retail investors, investor relations firms can be invaluable in identifying prospective institutional investors. But whether through outsourced means (investor relations firms) or internal means (directly approaching the institutional investors without third parties), targeting institutional investors often comes down to data. It's comparatively easy to tell which institutional investors own shares in industry peers and companies with similar capital markets profiles. Therefore, guesswork isn't needed concerning which institutional investors might have an interest in the company. Of course, investment funds are people, not machines, so that's where investor relations professionals (either internal or external) can add qualitative value.

- *Sell side.* The other predominant means of outreach to institutional investors is through sell-side equity research. Though discussed in far greater specificity in Chapter 10, equity research is critical for reaching institutional investors and creating more trading volume for one principal reason that many small-cap officers and directors don't sufficiently appreciate: once a stock is "under coverage," the analyst and the institutional sales personnel at the broker-dealer now have an incentive to increase the trading volume in the stock because any incremental trading volume (and the related trading commissions) traded through that broker-dealer represents incremental sell-side compensation. Therefore, as it pertains specifically to trading volume, equity research can be tremendously impactful on resource constrained small-cap companies, inasmuch as each broker-dealer who "covers" a stock also represents an indirect sales force for marketing the stock to institutional investors who aren't on the company's payroll.

The Sale

The company can have a great business, accurately identify who can realistically buy the company's stock, and take effective steps to reach investors, but there still isn't going to be an appreciable uptick in trading volume if the company (and its service providers) can't effectively sell stock. Like a lot of things that get obfuscated and needlessly complicated over time, the process of selling stock to either retail investors or institutions actually is not rocket science. Small-cap companies that have actively traded stocks over extended periods of time (1) have straightforward, understandable company presentations that are geared toward the audience; (2) set and achieve conservative expectations with investors; (3) answer questions succinctly and clearly; (4) have mechanisms for constructively keeping interested investors apprised of the company's progress; and (5) are responsive to follow-up inquiries in a timely fashion.

HOW SUSTAINABLE TRADING VOLUME IS *NOT* GENERATED

As important as it is for small-cap officers and directors to take appropriate steps to generate ample, sustainable trading volume, it's equally important for them to avoid common mistakes which don't achieve the objective.

Head in the Sand

Perhaps the most common, and worst, strategy for inactively traded small-cap companies is the, "We're just going to keep our heads down, deliver results, and the investors will find us" strategy. Even if the company operates in a sector that is hot and the company's revenues are growing quickly, this is a strategy that will not result in sustainable, ample trading volume. Sectors come in and out of favor, and while revenue growth will always attract attention, the vast majority of small-cap companies can't grow at breakneck speed forever. Therefore, sooner or later, company management is going to have to formulate a strategy to actively, constructively communicate with its target audience on the Street. Moreover, like a lot of things having to do with corporate finance and capital markets, it's a numbers game. That is, there are literally thousands of small-cap companies, so the head in the sand strategy is doomed on that basis alone. It's also worth noting that the head in the sand strategy is also not a wise strategy for companies to choose when things aren't going terribly well operationally, unless the company generates sufficient cash flow or it has cash reserves to sustain operations. Opting to cease any engagement with the Street when a company is performing poorly ("going dark") is likely to have two deleterious corporate finance consequences: (1) the company's trading volume will deteriorate to such an extent that the company will be prevented from raising equity capital; and (2) if the company is able to raise equity capital, the terms will be cripplingly dilutive.

Too Much of a Good Thing

There are small-cap management teams that take the opposite approach from the head in the sand strategy and often can end up with similar results. There are management teams that are incessantly on the road speaking to investors. But the law of diminishing returns applies to this situation for two reasons: (1) companies that continuously speak to investors can't possibly always have something new and material to report, so each meeting can be greeted with correspondingly less interest from investors; and (2) investors will begin to question who is running this small company while the CEO and CFO are crisscrossing the country every week speaking to investors.[14]

SPEAKING TO THE WRONG AUDIENCE

Almost every business day small-cap companies spend considerable amounts of money and management time meeting with institutional investors who can't (or won't) buy the company's stock. There are many reasons why this happens, and they are discussed in more detail in Part Three—Chapter 13. It suffices here to say that prior to meeting with any institutional investors, management should consider, at a minimum, answering one question: "Does this institution own any stock in substantially similar companies?" If the answer is no, then it's worth questioning whether such a meeting is a good use of time. This exercise applies to companies whether they have lots of institutional investors or none.

STOCK PROMOTERS

Small-cap officers and directors should approach any third parties that agree to increase the company's trading volume with circumspection. Because the goal for small-cap companies should be sustainable trading volume, not incidental or periodic spikes in trading volume, directors should make sure that management's analysis of any such third parties is focused on one critical question: "Can this vendor provide verifiable data showing increased, sustained trading volume for substantially similar companies?" Though it's hard to know precisely why, most veteran small-cap observers are mystified at how rarely this question is asked, and how rarely the answers are thoroughly verified.

SPAM

As discussed earlier, there are opt-in newsletters and opt-in digital outreach programs that are sensible for officers and directors to consider as part of an overall strategy to reach more retail investors. However, small-cap officers and directors should be circumspect about widespread e-mail or other digital campaigns that are not opt-in but rather are simply scattershot distributions to purchased mailing lists. While the reasons for such caution are self-explanatory, there are still a surprising number of small-cap companies that either authorize such distribution or indirectly authorize them by failing to appropriately supervise over-zealous service providers.

CONCLUSION

No matter how it's sliced, trading volume is critical to myriad small-cap companies.

Directors should focus on it and make sure, together with management, that there is a thoughtful, realistic strategy to achieve both near-term and longer-term liquidity objectives. Considering how seminal it is to so many elements of small-cap life, trading volume should actually be a metric that is regularly discussed and evaluated in the boardroom alongside other more familiar aspects of corporate performance.

Notes

1. There are certainly large-cap companies that many might agree should be valued at premiums to their peers. What's unique about an otherwise good-quality small-cap company that has *bad* stock is that such a company doesn't just run the risk of underperforming its peers; rather it runs the risk of disappearing. Although such a company might be operationally sound, there are scores of small-cap companies that for a variety of reasons that are discussed in Part Two toil in obscurity, with virtually illiquid stocks and no equity research coverage. These companies often run the real risk of not garnering sufficient growth capital to continue, while operationally less compelling companies might easily raise capital to live for another day.

2. The reality for many small-cap companies is that the equity markets are the likeliest path to raise appreciable capital considering that many small-cap companies, in the absence of material cash flow and fixed assets, aren't attractive to lenders.

3. Target liquidity in small-cap companies is tied to trading volumes that facilitate institutional ownership because institutional investors (as opposed to individual investors) ultimately are the driving force that propels small-cap companies to larger market capitalizations. In Chapter 10 there are some daily dollar trading thresholds discussed for equity research that are good proxies for target daily liquidity.

4. Directors who have predominantly mid- or large-cap capital markets experience often don't focus on the importance of trading volume because trading volume is simply not an issue for the majority of larger public companies. Moreover, if directors' capital markets experience is largely outside the small-cap realm, they also could

well have limited or no experience in the strategic steps necessary to increase trading volume.

5. See, Timothy J. Keating, *Aftermarket Support: How to Create a Liquid Public Stock*, http://keatingcapital.com/newsroom/white-papers/, 4, 5, 7 (statistics based upon data from Capital IQ, and updated in 2012).

6. Ibid., 4, 5, 7.

7. Ibid., 4. Keating Investments defines ADTV as the average number of shares traded daily (during the last twelve months) divided by the total number of shares outstanding at that time.

8. Some people would argue that one exception to this rule is, for example, the blockbuster drug approval for a previously unknown small-cap biotech company. But even that event-driven euphoria is unlikely to, in and of itself, provide sustainable trading volume.

9. Short-biased interest also creates trading volume and investor interest, but to a lesser degree in illiquid companies.

10. This is the reason why in the earlier statistical discussions, the median $100 million Nasdaq company institutional ownership is only 37 percent, and one in four such companies has no analyst coverage (i.e., where there aren't institutional investors, there isn't research coverage either).

11. The majority of institutional investors who buy and sell small-cap stocks in open market transactions (as opposed to in conjunction with a financing) focus on companies that are listed on national exchanges (e.g., Nasdaq, and NYSE).

12. Unless they are interested in effectuating corporate change, many institutional investors will not buy more than 9.99 percent of the issued and outstanding shares of a company because thereafter the investors will be considered "affiliates" or "insiders" and will be more restricted in their ability to buy and sell the company's stock. Moreover, there are also institutional investors who won't buy more than 4.99 percent of the issued and outstanding shares of a company because thereafter the investors needs to make public filings depicting their purchases and sales while their position stays above that threshold.

13. Investing preferences of investment funds (i.e., the types of companies in which funds usually invest and the amounts they invest) are typically known for two reasons: (a) there is a litany of proprietary databases containing granular information about thousands of funds; and (b) investment funds that have more than $100 million under management make publicly available quarterly filings pursuant to Section 13(f) of the Securities Exchange Act of 1934 indicating the stocks that are held.

14. This is often a serious concern because seasoned small-cap investors know that the annual number of investor meetings often can be inversely proportional to corporate performance.

CHAPTER 10

THE REALITIES OF SMALL-CAP EQUITY RESEARCH

Ins and Outs of Equity Research

Key considerations for directors:

- Small-cap directors need to understand the "business" of equity research if they are to help management garner and maintain research coverage.
- Notwithstanding how critical equity research is to many small-cap companies, many aren't credible candidates.
- Quality is more important than quantity, since not all research is created equal.
- Management needs to target analysts wisely, but also understand that anyone can write research on the company – good or bad.

Common mistakes to avoid:

- Management is often too impatient with the process of garnering coverage.
- Analysts aren't "friends" of the company; sell-side research is a business.
- Institutional sales people are vastly underutilized resources.
- Loose lips sink ships.

long with trading volume, equity research is critical to the evolution of small-cap companies. Equity research, like trading volume, isn't well understood by many small-cap officers and directors, and
it's also similarly elusive.

WHAT IS EQUITY RESEARCH?

As the name implies, equity research is a third-party–generated analysis of
a public company's strengths, weaknesses, market position, and prospective financial performance designed to induce or dissuade investors from
investing in the company's stock. There is typically a comprehensive initiation report followed by more succinct periodic updates that coincide with
quarterly earnings reports and other corporate events. The reports are typically produced by an individual or small team of industry experts. The
preparation of the reports (especially the initiation report) often, but not
always, includes management interviews and site visits. Generally speaking
there are three different sources of small-cap equity research:

- *Investment banks.* Equity research reports emanating from within
  the research divisions of full-service investment banks are the most
  common small-cap equity research and also the most impactful on the
  trading volume and share prices of small-cap stocks. The research is
  distributed predominantly in electronic format to client institutional
  investors and retail investors (usually through the issuing bank's
  wealth management division). Institutional and retail investors don't
  typically pay for the equity research reports, per se, but the issuing
  banks receive indirect revenue associated with the reports.[1]

- *Client-paid research boutiques.* Equity research boutiques differ
  from full-service investment banks because they principally focus
  on producing equity research reports and then selling that research
  predominantly to investment funds for a fee.[2] Research boutiques
  are often focused on certain industries and are also often either

long-biased or short-biased. Rather than focus on lesser-known small-cap companies, research boutiques frequently try to create value for their clients by contributing unique viewpoints on larger, more well-known companies.

- *Issuer-paid research boutiques.* Small-cap companies that are either too inactively traded, nascent, or otherwise challenged often don't attract the attention of investment banks or research boutiques and instead sometimes elect to pay independent research firms to produce reports. In much the same way that large-issuer–paid credit reporting agencies are subject to withering scrutiny because of the perceived conflicts of interest, issuer-paid research coverage similarly struggles with such credibility issues. Though there are vendors known for producing substantially unbiased reports, issuer-paid research often isn't materially impactful on small-cap stock prices or trading volumes.

WHY INVESTMENT BANKS ISSUE EQUITY RESEARCH

While it's hard to find a small-cap officer or director who has never read an equity research report, a surprising number don't sufficiently understand the business case for equity research. Without a firm understanding of why it makes sense for investment banks to offer equity research, it's more challenging for small-cap companies to excel at garnering and maintaining research coverage, and it's also more difficult for them to understand the motivations of equity analysts.

Trading in Covered Names

Equity research analysts are typically paid a salary, but often an element of their compensation is variable. The variable component is derived from stock trading commissions earned by the bank's institutional sales people with respect to companies under coverage and bonuses essentially resulting from the accuracy and performance of the analyst's recommendations.[3] In short, the less equity research results in trading through the issuing investment bank and the less accurate the analyst's predictions, the less money the analyst makes, and the less money the investment bank makes.

ANCILLARY REVENUE STREAMS

Equity research, while independent of other investment banking functions, indirectly generates revenue and increases an investment bank's ability to differentiate itself from its peers. Equity research can assist investment bankers in garnering fee-generating banking business; it can assist the bank in earning fee-generating mergers and acquisition advisory business; and it can also assist, attract, and retain wealth management clients. In short, timely, accurate, and reliable equity research drives a lot more than just trading commissions at investment banks.

EQUITY RESEARCH IS CRITICAL FOR SMALL-CAP COMPANIES

As alluded to elsewhere in this book, equity research is critically important to small-cap companies for a variety of interrelated reasons:

- *Introduction and validation.* For small-cap companies that have no equity research coverage, the initiation of that coverage represents the "introduction" of that company, and a validation that the company is ready for consideration by institutional investors. While the more trusted and revered the source of the research coverage, the more impactful the initiation for the company, the first piece of equity research on a small-cap company is often a sign of credibility (especially if the initiation report encourages investors to buy the stock).

- *Operating model.* Especially if it's the first equity research report issued on a small-cap company, the operating model contained in the first report (along with its assumptions and forecasts) is among the most valuable elements of the research because it creates a framework to help institutional investors analyze and evaluate the newly covered company without building the model from scratch themselves. Moreover, even if it's not the first research report, institutional investors look to trusted research analysts to provide them with a more astute analysis of the business model than might have been provided by previous research analysts.

- *Trading volume, price, and heightened exposure.* As discussed in Chapter 9, equity research generates more trading volume for small-cap companies because the issuing bank's institutional salespeople have an incentive to have their clients trade the stock of companies under coverage. While not all equity research is optimistic about a covered company's prospects, research that is undertaken by a respected analyst and offers a bullish forecast for a company's prospects can certainly be impactful on a company's stock price both in the near and longer term. Additionally, small-cap companies with equity research coverage also have opportunities to further increase their visibility with strategic partners, institutional investors, and other equity analysts that small-cap companies without research coverage conspicuously lack. That is, investment banks often invite companies under coverage (especially those with bullish prospects) to make presentations at coveted investor conferences and also arrange "nondeal investor roadshows" where the company is typically escorted by the analyst and/or institutional sales personnel to meet with both existing and new institutional investors.[4]

- *Research begets more research.* One of the hardest parts of securing the initial research coverage for a small-cap company is that there is both brand and financial risk associated with being the first one. After each successive bank initiates research coverage, these risks fade. Therefore, equity research coverage of small-cap companies tends to result in more equity research coverage.

HOW TO ATTRACT EQUITY
RESEARCH COVERAGE

It's important for small-cap directors to understand the basics of attracting equity research coverage so that they can assess whether management is appropriately pursuing equity research or whether the company is even a credible candidate for research coverage. As is the case with much in the small-cap ecosystem, some of the steps are intuitive, and some aren't.

No Visibility, No Research Coverage

Officers and directors often confuse a bright future with visibility, but the two are very different. Nascent businesses are typically not candidates for credible equity research coverage because forward-looking operating models (and resulting valuations) that are the cornerstone of equity research reports require revenue, expense, and earnings visibility. In other words, if management doesn't have confidence in a 12-month operating model, then how can equity research analysts feel comfortable when they aren't even privy to material, nonpublic information? Companies with insufficient historic operations and forward-looking operating visibility are not good candidates for equity research, ebullient prospects notwithstanding. Officers and directors need to be brutally realistic in this regard, lest they waste a lot of time and risk damaging the company's credibility by proactively seeking research coverage prematurely.

No Trading Volume, No Research Coverage

Even if a company is otherwise strong operationally and has excellent visibility, trading volume in the company's stock is almost always a prerequisite for equity research coverage because if institutional clients can't buy the stock, then there will be no resulting trading commissions for the initiating investment bank.[5] More specifically, the **key point** here for officers and directors is that smaller, regional investment banks often won't initiate research coverage on small-cap companies with stock that trades less than $250,000 per day, and larger, national investment banks won't initiate research coverage on small-cap companies with stock that trades less than $1 million per day. This further underscores the points made in Chapter 9 with respect to the overall importance of trading volume.

START SOMEWHERE

For small-cap companies with no research coverage, the principal challenge is getting an analyst to be the first to cover the stock—you have to start somewhere. Analysts have to be convinced that there is merit to the story at the current valuation and money to be made for clients. The easiest and best place for management to begin making constructive inroads in this regard is to first pinpoint the analysts who write research on peer companies.[6] Sometimes analysts might not express material interest in the company, but, at a minimum, they might begin to at least discuss the company indirectly as part of the narrative in other research reports. It's also important for management to be mindful of the fact that the first research initiation can have as much to do with personal and professional rapport as it does with company acumen. In order for analysts to take a chance on a company with no research coverage, there often are intangibles that contribute to the decision as much as quantitative justifications do. Therefore, management needs to not only target analysts who cover similarly situated companies, but it also needs to patiently let relationships develop.

TIP

One of the reasons why it's hard to overemphasize a thorough understanding of the business case for equity research is because small-cap companies often need to strategically utilize all the sell-side machinations to their advantage in order to, among other things, attract research coverage. That is, if a small-cap company doesn't have any research coverage but it is going to undertake an equity financing imminently or engage in some mergers and acquisition ("M&A") activity, those are exactly the type of fee-generating events that investment banks relish. Therefore, whenever small-cap companies (that are otherwise suitable candidates for equity research) have imminent fee-generating banking events, directors should make sure that officers are constructively leveraging this to secure research coverage. As discussed in Chapter 3, even in such situations of leverage, officers and directors still need to do their best to pick the bank where the analyst is not only favorably inclined to the company, but where the institutional sales group has a demonstrated track record of supporting substantially similar companies.

TARGETING ADDITIONAL ANALYSTS

Once the company has equity research coverage, the process of adding more research analysts should be more about quality than quantity. The best use of management's time involves seeking out analysts who have the most credibility with institutional investors.[7] While the company might not be large enough to be a credible candidate for coverage with all the industry's leading analysts, the board needs to make sure that officers have a strategy to identify and pursue coverage from the most influential analysts who would consider covering the company. And relationships take time to develop; therefore, management needs to be patient and mindful of the constraints under which some analysts operate.[8]

NOT ALL RESEARCH IS CREATED EQUAL

Many small-cap companies spend so much time in pursuit of equity research coverage that they lose sight of the fact that more research coverage isn't necessarily better. Some equity research (and institutional sales groups) can be impactful on a small-cap company, while other research is of little consequence. Considering how excessively time consuming it can be for management to help research analysts get up to speed on the company, answer due diligence inquiries, and assist analysts with modeling the company's business, boards need to be vigilant about the opportunity costs of poor choices given the typically constrained resources of small-cap companies.

Moreover, a fact that's less appreciated by some inexperienced small-cap officers and directors is that equity research isn't only something that's sought. Rather it can "find" the company. That is, as long as equity research reports aren't intentionally false and misleading (or otherwise not in compliance with applicable laws and regulations), virtually any third-party can write and distribute equity research about the company. But just because equity research analysts want management's time and resources in anticipation of initiating coverage doesn't always make it the best use of management's efforts.

COMMON MANAGEMENT MISTAKES

Considering the importance of attracting and maintaining equity research coverage for small-cap companies, directors should be mindful of common mistakes that are made in this regard:

- *Impatience.* As in all personal and business relationships, hounding or stalking equity research analysts rarely lays the foundation for a good relationship. Sometimes, mindful of how impactful equity research coverage can be on the company from a particular analyst, inexperienced small-cap officers simply get carried away in their pursuit of these analysts. As it is a common occurrence, and typically all but ends the possibility of research coverage from the target analyst (or from others with whom the company's actions are shared), directors should be cognizant of this possibility and take appropriate steps to avoid it.

- *Loose lips.* High-quality equity research analysts won't respect management or the company if conversations regularly violate Regulation FD. Inexperienced small-cap officers often feel that providing analysts with "extra" insight into the business will garner more complimentary recommendations, but management's inclination to share material nonpublic information deters high-quality analysts. Directors should remind officers where appropriate to always stick to information that's 100 percent public.

- *Arm's length.* It's common for management teams to develop a close rapport with equity research analysts over the course of time. It's critical for boards to remind sometimes inexperienced small-cap management that analysts are definitely not "friends" of management or the company in the playground sense. That is, equity research is a high-stakes business in which all the parties involved are best served by maintaining arm's length relationships. From the sell-side perspective, research is time consuming and puts reputations at risk; when money isn't being made, relationships either end or recommendations change in order to restore profit and reputations. Management that confuses positive research recommendations with friendship might unwittingly create a conflict of interest at best, or exercise judgment that negatively impacts shareholders at worst.

- *Just say no.* As discussed earlier, there are helpful, high-quality equity research analysts who cover small-cap stocks, and there are the opposite. Boards need to make sure that management isn't spending time and effort responding to analysts who have poor or unhelpful reputations, lest they inhibit the company's ability to attract and maintain research coverage from higher-quality analysts.[9] For example, analysts frequently request customer references; customers will reluctantly agree to speak periodically with equity analysts, but are leery of the time and the dangers associated with unintended disclosures of sensitive information. If a company isn't judicious about its review of analyst acumen, it risks alienating important future customer references because of overzealous questioning by unskilled or disingenuous analysts.

- *Don't lose sight of sell-side business.* One of the principal foundations for successful sell-side relationships is making sure that management never loses sight of how the sell-side makes money. Especially with inexperienced small-cap management, emotions need to always take a back seat to the business of equity research. For example, rather than reacting negatively to initiations, recommendations, and price targets, small-cap companies need to objectively focus on how the company's actions or omissions might have impacted the sell-side's ability to make money from research. Moreover, investment banks make money from fee-generating events like financings and M&A; therefore, companies need to always be vigilant about making sure to reward banks with helpful analysts by including them in transactions. The **key point** here for small-cap officers and directors is that they need to be holistic in how they approach and react to the company's sell-side relationships, and they also need to realize that fee-generating events are opportunities to further cement relationships which have generated value for shareholders.

• *Outreach.* Institutional sales personnel who work with well-respected analysts are literally treasure troves of information about the company's strengths, weaknesses, and investor perceptions. Unfortunately, small-cap management rarely takes advantage of the opportunity to periodically spend time with the salespeople, listen to their feedback, and arm them with ways in which to respond to investor concerns. Institutional sales people are on the front lines daily interfacing with institutional investors, and the better they understand the company and the more they trust management, the better the job they will do on the company's behalf.

• *Just the facts.* Like institutional investors, equity research analysts and institutional sales people are exceedingly good listeners and take precise notes. Therefore, small-cap officers are well advised to: (1) never let their guard down; (2) speak carefully and factually; (3) avoid speculation and extraneous details; and (4) if they don't know the answer to a question, admit it and make sure the question gets answered as quickly as possible. Especially less-experienced management needs to be carefully monitored in this regard.

CONCLUSION

Equity research is so critical to most small-cap companies that directors need to not only better understand the business of equity research but also be prepared to help management avoid all the common mistakes made in garnering and maintaining equity research.

Notes

1. This chapter focuses predominantly on equity research issued by investment banks.

2. In other words, they typically don't have extensive investment banking, mergers and acquisition advisory, trading, and wealth management services.

3. Investment banks have institutional sales people that cover different investment funds and portfolio managers. The goal of institutional salespeople is to build a trusted rapport with investors concerning the companies under coverage at the investment bank. As a reward for that trust (and related trust in the equity research), institutional investors will often route their trades in a particular stock through the trusted institutional salesperson and pay a commission for the trade execution.

4. Other than travel expenses, these events are typically offered at no charge to the company. Investment banks have conferences and organize road shows because they not only cement the relationships between investors and the investment bank and companies and the investment bank, but they also help to further drive trading revenue and the ancillary revenue streams discussed previously. The added exposure at comparatively minimal expense is especially important to small-cap companies given their routinely constrained balance sheets.

5. It's worth noting that there are a small number of small-cap focused investment banks that initiate equity research coverage on inactively traded stocks because they have a handful of institutional investor clients who are willing to patiently acquire shares under the right circumstances. These firms are definitely in the minority.

6. When trying to interest analysts in covering a company with no research, it's important to look for analysts that have not shied away from doing so in the past or that have companies under coverage that have similar capital markets profiles. That is, if an analyst is highly respected but only has larger, more seasoned companies under coverage, then it's less likely that such an analyst will have an interest.

7. Analyst credibility is relatively easy to discern over the course of time spent speaking about them with institutional investors. Additionally, publications like *Institutional Investor Magazine* and *The Wall Street Journal* provide analyst rankings.

8. In addition to either tacit or bright line trading volume thresholds, many analysts can't write research on companies with stocks that trade below $5, or

sometimes even $10, and most will write research only on companies listed on national exchanges (e.g., NYSE and Nasdaq).

9. To be clear, analysts intent on covering a particular stock are going to do so with or without management's cooperation. The point here is that cooperation and the extent of cooperation are elective and should be directly proportional to the quality of the analyst (and the analyst's firm).

CHAPTER 11

AVOIDING MISTAKES WHEN COMMUNICATING WITH THE STREET

Street Communication 101

Key considerations for directors:

- Poor Street communication practices can be especially penal for small-cap companies.
- Eight basic tenets comprise the core of prudent Street communication.
- Overpromising and underdelivering are hard for small-cap companies to recover from.
- When in doubt, just stick to the facts.
- Don't hide from or try to disguise bad news.
- Be as transparent as possible about the things investors care about.

Common mistakes to avoid:

- Issuing immaterial press releases.
- Talking over investors' heads.
- Providing either no business outlook or guidance that's intentionally inaccurate ("sandbagging").
- Dignifying Internet gobbledygook with a reply.
- Being poorly prepared for quarterly earnings calls.
- Lacking an enforceable social media policy, or having no policy at all.

I n medical school, aspiring doctors often spend the first year learning how the human body is supposed to work under optimal circumstances, and they spend the remaining three years learning how it falls apart. Similarly, the conventional wisdom governing how small-cap companies should best communicate with the Street is fairly straightforward, while the extent of the mistakes made could easily fill a separate book.

What's particularly important for directors to discuss with their colleagues is that the ramifications of poor communication practices are considerably more austere for small-cap companies than they are for larger companies. Unlike larger public companies where only crisis communications have substantive enterprise risk, daily communications with the Street can result in dire enterprise risk for many small-cap companies which are reliant on investor sentiment, stock price, and trading volume to facilitate further infusions of growth capital. For small-cap companies there is a direct correlation between poor Street communications practices on the one hand and availability and cost of capital on the other.

Therefore, the purpose of this chapter is to discuss some standard axioms of communicating with the Street, and then apply them to a wide range of common small-cap scenarios in order to suggest some different approaches for officers and directors to consider.

AXIOMS OF COMMUNICATING WITH THE STREET[1]

Invariably, when small-cap companies communicate poorly with the Street, it's because one or more of the following tenets were compromised:

1. *Audience.* As alluded to in Chapter 6, all communication should be geared to the intended audience, and communicating with the Street is no exception. When this axiom is disregarded in

small-cap circles, it typically results in people talking over the heads of retail investors, or speaking past just about everyone other than industry cognoscenti in situations involving highly complex technology or science.

2. *Set realistic expectations.* If there could be only one tenet governing communications between small-cap companies and investors, it would likely be this golden rule: don't overpromise and underdeliver. Yet, this is one of the most common mistakes in the small-cap ecosystem.[2] The challenges for most officers and directors occur in connection with providing quarterly and yearly financial guidance.

3. *Stick to the facts.* When in doubt, all written and oral communications with the Street should be factual; that is, the less hyperbole, speculation, or extraneous commentary the better. Small-cap management teams tend to run into trouble in this area, especially during extemporaneous question-and-answer sessions with investors (e.g., investor meetings, conference presentations, earnings calls, etc.).

4. *Press releases are for material news.* The best rule of thumb for small-cap companies is that press releases disseminated through wire services should be limited to material information only—hype should be considered a four-letter word. Next to overpromising and underdelivering, small-cap company hype erodes investor confidence the most.

5. *Strive for transparency.* Small-cap companies should strive to provide the maximum transparency possible[3] with respect to issues that investors are most concerned about. Small-cap companies are risky enough propositions for investors already; asking them to operate in the dark with respect to seminal data and dispositive issues is unlikely to attract and retain them. This

issue typically comes up in conjunction with investor meetings and earnings communications.

6. *Handle bad news directly.* Just as people often measure one another by how they respond to adversity, the same is true for small-cap investors and the companies in which they invest. It's inevitable that small-cap companies will have setbacks; officers and directors can go a long way toward mitigating the impact of bad news by addressing shortfalls frankly and directly. Unfortunately, many small-cap companies choose obfuscation over clarity, especially in connection with earnings communications.

7. *Proactive versus reactive.* Wherever possible, investor concerns should be addressed proactively as opposed to reactively; that is, when a call or press release discussing quarterly results addresses investor concerns before they are actually raised, it inspires confidence that management understands what matters most to investors.

8. *Be wary of precedents.* Small-cap companies must always be vigilant about communications with the Street that might set a precedent for additional similar communication. This situation typically arises when management elects to comment on unusual occurrences, third-party commentary, market innuendo. or company performance.

Although there are many situations that arise between public companies and investors, small-cap companies have somewhat unusual interactions with investors because management are far more accessible, and many large investors in small-cap companies have met personally with management, sometimes on numerous occasions. In addition to accessibility and personal rapport, small-cap officers are also often considerably more deferential to investors than are officers in larger public company settings because investor happiness is critical to the ability of many small-cap companies to continue to garner infusions of outside capital. The **key point** here for officers and directors is that institutional investors, mindful of this leverage, often utilize their rapport with management to "encourage" small-cap companies to take (or not take) actions that are helpful to the investors.[4] Sometimes, the proposed actions or omissions are prudent and consistent with building long-term value for shareholders, and sometimes investors' suggestions serve only one purpose—to help boost volume or the share price in the short term for the financial benefit of the investors.[5] The challenge for directors is to assist management with balancing what is heard from investors while developing and adhering to prudent Street communications practices.

Directors should be mindful of the common small-cap communications challenges set forth below and should consider using some of the observations to foster constructive dialogue with management about possible alternative approaches.

NONFINANCIAL PRESS RELEASES

MATERIALITY

- *Situation.* The company's stock price and/or trading volume is depressed, and management is being pressured to issue press releases with greater frequency in order to give investors a reason to buy the stock. Although the company doesn't have a sufficient flow of material news, it instead begins to issue press releases about immaterial news and events in order to stay in front of investors.

- *Different approach.* While issuing press releases can certainly create near-term increases in stock price and trading volume—especially in companies with predominantly retail investor bases—press releases devoid of material news don't create long-lasting change in stock price or trading volume and could well accomplish the opposite of the desired effect.[6] Moreover, small-cap companies that frequently issue press releases containing immaterial information run the risk of denigrating investor trust to such an extent that when the company releases impactful news, the company will suffer consequences akin to the boy who cried wolf. Therefore, companies with an unpredictable flow of material information should consider regularly posting instructive information about the company and its industry (i.e., white papers, videos, etc.) on the company's website and encourage interested investors to regularly check there for updates. This way, the company can remain engaging and proactive without risking a conspicuous loss of investor trust.

SCIENCE AND TECHNOLOGY

- *Situation*. There are many small-cap companies involved in technology or science that have products and services that are highly technical. Some small-cap companies simply assume that their investors understand what the company does (otherwise they wouldn't be investors), and therefore there is no reason to issue press releases with easily understandable "lay" terminology. Other small-cap companies feel that the way to attract highly technical investors who are best suited to understanding the company's value proposition is to write press releases for that audience (i.e., impress existing and prospective investors with the company's technical acumen). Therefore, more often than not, technology- and science-focused small-cap companies issue highly technical press releases.

- *Different approach*. Both of these approaches are rarely effective for small-cap companies because both of them overestimate the audience's technical acumen. Just because retail investors buy the stock of a biotechnology company doesn't mean that they understand molecular nano-compounds any more than an institutional investor understands optical modulator technology.

Consequently, most small-cap companies are considerably better off reserving technical terminology for responding to similarly technical inbound investor inquiries. They should explain what the company does in the ordinary course of its business in plain English so that it's readily understandable to the vast majority of investors. A good exercise for officers and directors is simply to hand a recent product press release to an uninitiated third party and see whether this person is able to understand it. Being too technical is an enormous problem in the small-cap ecosystem, and directors should work together with management to make sure that, at a minimum, investors understand what the company does.

Less Is More

- *Situation.* The company is going to announce some important news and is eager to make sure that investors view the news as important. In order to drive the point home, the text of the press release includes language like, "We are unbelievably excited to release this game-changer!"

- *Different approach.* Small-cap companies routinely try to fill press releases with superlatives, modifiers, and exclamation points, but at best this approach is not impactful, and at worst it can be viewed as so novice and unprofessional that it actually takes away from an otherwise compelling piece of news. Directors should advise management that when in doubt, just let the facts speak for themselves. For example, there is a reason why you don't see Fortune 500 companies using that language or resorting to exclamation points in press releases.

Partnerships

- *Situation.* A small-cap company has entered into a partnership with a larger well-known company that has potentially compelling business possibilities for the smaller company. The relationship isn't material to the larger company, and it's unwilling to provide any quotes for the smaller company's press release and unwilling to enter into a joint release. Moreover, the economic impacts of the relationship, though likely to be material to the smaller company, are challenging to estimate. In order to drive home the significance of the new relationship and make up for the lack of quotes or involvement from the larger company, the small-cap company issues a press release that touts the likely financial impact of the relationship (without providing any specific details), and conveys that the relationship is transformative.

- *Different approach.* Investors' reactions to press releases like these (which are very common) are typically two-fold: (1) If it's such an important partnership, why won't the other company comment about it? (2) If it's so transformative, why can't the company provide investors with some guidance on the business case? In other words, investors tend to view these types of announcements differently from the way the companies intend them to be viewed. Therefore, small-cap companies in these situations should consider being patient and just sticking to the facts. That way, if the partnership turns out to be transformative, then the financial results will speak for themselves in due course, and if it doesn't, the company won't have risked damaging its credibility with investors by setting unrealistic expectations. The **key point** here for directors is that management needs to understand that experienced small-cap investors typically take a wait and see approach to partnerships between diminutive small-cap companies and Fortune 500 companies for good reason—and management should also.

Blogs and Third-Party Commentary

- *Situation.* The company receives a positive endorsement from a product reviewer, industry publication, television show, or stock blogger and decides to put the endorsement into a press release because the company would like to make sure that the endorsement is seen by a large audience.

- *Different approach.* First and foremost, this is a question of materiality; that is, endorsements, unless they actually contain real news about the company, are rarely relevant in and of themselves.[7] Rather than risk damaging the company's credibility with investors in an effort to create a spike in trading volume or the share price, the company should consider putting this type of information on the company's website (if anywhere), and save press releases for substantive news only.

FINANCIAL PRESS RELEASES

Titles and Subtitles

- *Scenario.* A company is going to report quarterly financial results that do not meet the expectations the company and equity research analysts predicted. It elects to highlight in the title and subtitle of its earnings press release that the company had a record number of new customer wins and that the company won a prestigious industry award; the company is trying to offset the poor financial results by accentuating other positive developments.

- *Different approach.* With decidedly few exceptions, most investors (including retail investors) care about only seminal data when it comes to earnings releases (revenue, margins, cash balances, clinical trials progress, earnings per share, forward guidance, etc). Therefore, trying to obfuscate those data in an earnings release is ineffectual at best and at worst could cause investors to question management's judgment. While there is nothing wrong with a company putting its proverbial best foot forward, small-cap officers and directors should carefully weigh focusing upon noncore financial results in earnings releases. Instead, when facing this common small-cap situation, companies should consider addressing the disappointing results frankly and directly.

CONSISTENCY

- *Scenario.* A company traditionally reports its quarterly results and always compares the latest results to the same quarter in the prior year. Its impending quarterly results show no growth over the same period in the prior year, but revenues are up dramatically over the immediately preceding quarter. In order to augment shareholder reaction to the otherwise lackluster year over year results, the company decides to change the way it traditionally reports and to highlight only the sequential growth.

- *Different approach.* The methodology a company uses to report quarterly financial results needs to be consistent from quarter to quarter and within each earnings release. While retail investors might not notice the inconsistencies (because it's not their profession to read hundreds of earnings releases), institutional investors will notice, and they will quickly surmise the intentions. This comes down to the axiom stated in the beginning of this chapter with which small-cap companies routinely struggle— handling bad news directly. Very rarely does anything good come from a public company's failure to handle disappointing news frankly and directly.[8]

TRANSPARENCY

- *Situation.* A company has multiple product segments, all of which have different margin profiles. The company's fastest-growing product, and the product for which the company is best known, has the lowest gross margins of all its products. Although the company isn't overly concerned about competitors knowing the margins for that product, it doesn't want to break out the product's margins, because investors will be concerned that the company's future is tied to lower-margin products. The company continues to resist releasing this information, despite myriad investor requests.

• *Different approach*. Small-cap officers and directors often underestimate that in the small-cap ecosystem companies need investors a lot more than investors need companies. Small-cap companies are risky enough to begin with, and investors are more than happy to move on to other opportunities if they can't get sufficient financial granularity on issues they deem seminal to assessing risk and reward. Consequently, officers and directors should consider providing the transparency investors seek with respect to the issues that matter most to them, subject to material competitive concerns. The alternative is that sooner or later investors will vote with their feet.

TIP

One of the most overlooked tools at the disposal of small-cap officers and directors for determining whether there is confusion about company messaging or dissatisfaction with financial reporting are investor message boards (in particular, widely used one's like Yahoo! Finance). Message boards are also routinely venues for scams and half-truths designed to push stock prices up or down. However, it's a mistake for small-cap companies to completely ignore what's said in those forums (especially for companies with no analyst coverage, and thus no institutional sales people to provide such feedback) because mixed in with the "ne'er do wells" are investors that are genuinely interested in the company and follow it closely. Therefore, there are typically valuable insights to be had by occasionally skimming the comments in order to discern themes and trends especially directly before and after investor conferences and quarterly earnings reports.

GUIDANCE

- *Scenario 1.* A company has a relatively nascent, growing business with minimal visibility as to revenue growth. Rather than risk setting unattainable expectations, the company doesn't provide any forward-looking guidance in its earnings press release, and reiterates its "no guidance" policy in response to investor inquiries on the company's quarterly earnings call.

- *Different approach.* As said at the beginning of this chapter, overpromising and underdelivering is a cardinal sin for small-cap companies. Therefore, the company can't be faulted for its sensitivity to this. However, what an investor hears when a company says, "Our policy is to not provide any guidance," is either, "We're lying to you," or, "We have no idea what's going on in our business." Neither of these assumptions is good for investors or the company. Therefore, officers and directors should at least consider a middle ground where the company tries to provide some information to investors but doesn't go so far as to set unrealistic expectations. For example, even companies without clear visibility might be able to tell with confidence that revenue is going to grow each quarter, they just don't know by how much. Or perhaps the company is confident because it has a contract in the final stages of negotiations. When the contract is final, gross margins are expected to increase a bit each quarter or for the whole year. Or maybe the company knows that a "cost plus" drug manufacturing contract with the government is likely to provide the company with positive cash flow for the year, but the company just doesn't know by how much. Regardless of the circumstances, investors will welcome the company's attempt to provide some transparency even if the commentary doesn't qualify as "guidance" in the way that many might think of guidance. Of course, if the company simply lacks sufficient visibility to offer any forward-looking commentary, then silence is likely the best policy unless or until visibility improves.

- *Scenario 2.* A company has sufficient visibility to provide revenue and margin guidance and decides to provide ranges for each that it is confident the company will surpass by at least 25 percent in order to impress upon analysts and investors how well the company is performing.

- *Different approach.* A famous dog trainer once told students that the only thing you accomplish by telling your dog to sit ten times instead of once is that the dog doesn't need to listen to you the first time. Similarly, "sandbagging" financial guidance rarely achieves the objective because over time this approach will only succeed in teaching investors that your guidance is inaccurate. Worse still, analysts will move their models and targets higher to reflect the company's historic overachievement, and then the company will be at risk of missing consensus numbers instead of easily surpassing them. The **key point** here for directors is that artificially lowering financial guidance will ultimately penalize the company should its performance actually fall within the provided range. Instead, officers and directors should consider providing guidance ranges that reflect the company's internal plan numbers toward the top of the range. This way, the company has a cushion on the downside and also impresses on analysts and investors that the company's guidance is an accurate reflection of what the company expects to achieve.

PREANNOUNCEMENT

- *Scenario.* A company's stock price is under pressure, and the company is being encouraged to preannounce its earnings if the results are even slightly better than consensus estimates in order to provide some impetus for the stock to trade higher in the near term.

- *Different approach.* Investor goading notwithstanding, preannouncing earnings is a precarious practice for public companies primarily because of the precedent that it might set.

If the company preannounces under the circumstances mentioned above but doesn't preannounce in the next quarter or in the quarter after that, investors are likely to conclude each time (rightfully or wrongfully) that in the absence of a positive preannouncement, the results will probably not be good. This not only risks diminishing investor confidence, but it also increases volatility in the stock— neither of which is good. Therefore, officers and directors should approach preannouncement with a healthy degree of caution and exercise care to consider preannouncements principally when the variance in expected results is highly material.

INTERNET REPORTS AND MARKET INNUENDO

At one point or another, most small-cap companies will be the subject of a bearish blog published on a financial website or assorted rumors that give rise to volatile stock trading. Directors should encourage management to be cautious about how, or if, they publicly respond to such matters.[9]

SHORT BLOG

- *Situation.* A sensationalized blog post from an obscure or anonymous source is entered on a financial website that insinuates that the company is either misleading investors or perpetrating a fraud; the stock price is dropping precipitously. The company maintains that the claims being made are false and damaging and elects to issue a press release addressing what the blog said in order to restore the company's credibility and put a halt to the stock price decline.

- *Different approach.* This is an increasingly common and sometimes sinister scenario[10] that can cause dramatic and immediate problems for a small-cap company. Cool heads need to prevail under such circumstances, and officers and directors should be mindful of the fact that the company might well be judged as much by the company's response as by the credibility of the blog post. Therefore, if the company is already covered by equity research, it might want to converse with its most influential analyst to see if the analyst would consider issuing a report responding to the blog post in lieu of a company press release. There are three reasons why this would be preferable to the company issuing its own press release: (1) the company risks dignifying the blog post with more credibility than it's otherwise due by responding to it; (2) if the blog post is from an anonymous source (as some of the most inflammatory are), a direct reply is tantamount to tilting at windmills; and (3) the company runs the risk of establishing a dangerous precedent by publicly replying.[11] If the company doesn't have any equity research coverage (or if existing analysts don't feel inclined to comment on the blog post), then the company might alternatively consider proactively addressing the concerns directly by phone with the company's largest shareholders (subject to Regulation FD). Additionally, and if the company feels that the blog post has created some legitimate confusion among existing or prospective investors, the company could also consider clarifying the content of the post during the company's next regularly scheduled earnings call without actually referencing the blog post by name.

TIP

As discussed in Chapter 2, the topic of short selling can occupy an inordinate amount of time among small-cap officers and directors, partially because short selling is widely misunderstood:

- In order to short a stock, an investor needs to be able to borrow the shares. If the shares are not borrowable from stock loan desks at broker-dealers, then the stock can't be shorted (unless it's sold without first borrowing the shares, also known as "naked shorting"). Well less than 1 percent of the daily dollar trading volume in the United States is estimated to be the result of naked shorting.

- For many small-cap stocks that are not institutionally owned, the cost of borrowing stock can be prohibitively expensive, if it's even available.
- If a stock is inactively traded, it's equally hard to buy or sell short.
- If a small-cap stock is expensive to borrow, then the short-seller needs to make more money from the trade than might otherwise be necessary to cover the borrowing expense.

The **key point** here for officers and directors is that very often small-cap companies (especially those not traded on national exchanges) get fixated on short-selling conspiracy theories when the decrease in the stock price might be more attributable to there simply being more sellers than buyers. More specifically, if the company's stock is illiquid, low-priced, and hard to borrow, then material short-selling is unlikely.

For small-cap companies listed on national exchanges where short interest is more easily confirmed, a rising short interest should trigger some hard questions for the board in lieu of malevolence: (1) Is the company doing a good job of communicating with the Street? (2) Does management have a credibility problem? (3) What other steps can be taken to optimize the company's performance or financial reporting? (4) If all the company's peers have similarly growing short interests, then what can the company do to hedge the industry exposure or distinguish itself from its peer group?

INNUENDO

- *Situation.* A biotech company's stock is trading at four times its normal volume and is down 50 percent intraday on rumors that its Phase III clinical trial was unsuccessful. The company, seeking to quell the rumor and decrease the rumor's impact on its stock price, elects to issue a press release stating that the rumor is not true.

- *Different approach.* Especially given the role that the Internet plays in circulating information (and misinformation) about small-cap stocks, rumors and innuendo can be as commonplace as facts. Consequently, directors should encourage officers to consider whether the benefit of responding to such rumors by press release outweighs the precedent being set by responding to the rumors. Moreover, it might also be a good exercise to quickly examine the stock charts of peer companies that were recently beset by market-moving rumors and see what happened to the stocks of companies in which the rumors were false and the companies didn't respond. Many times stocks targeted by innuendo correct themselves naturally in due course.

EARNINGS CALLS

Earnings calls arguably have a heightened degree of importance in the small-cap ecosystem. Many small-cap management teams are relatively new to shepherding publicly traded companies, and management performance on earnings calls can be highly variable. Moreover, the consequences of making a poor impression on earnings calls can be more penal for many small-cap companies than for large-cap companies given the need to frequently access the equity capital markets.

Directors should consider helping management avoid some of these common problems:

- *Preparation.* Whether the input for earnings calls comes from shareholders, analysts, management, investor relations professionals, or Internet message boards, companies need to prepare for all the (hard) questions that investors are likely to ask and have accurate, succinct, understandable answers that are consistent with management's prior statements. Arguably nothing differentiates seasoned, credible public company officers from neophytes more than their ability to calmly and expertly answer investor questions. Although some of that skill certainly comes with experience, a great deal of it comes from preparation.

- *Speakerphone.* Most management teams make earnings calls from a conference room where they are together using a speakerphone. The company should always make sure to have others listen first to the acoustics of the room and phone prior to using them for an earnings call. Seasoned small-cap investors often marvel at how regularly they have to struggle to hear what management is saying. Furthermore, managers need to remind each other before such calls to exercise appropriate speakerphone protocol; that is, they need to wait for others to finish speaking before they respond so that the speakerphone will not cancel out the voices altogether. These issues are intuitive, but regularly take place at many small-cap companies.

- *Call scripts.* Whether or not officers prepare their own call scripts or have someone else prepare the scripts for them, there is no excuse for failing to sufficiently rehearse the script. More specifically, when officers struggle through their scripts or sound like they are awkwardly reading something that they've never seen before, it erodes investor confidence in the message. Although this seems intuitive also, it's a surprisingly common problem—a problem that few small-cap companies can really afford to make.

- *Proactive action.* Earnings calls are good opportunities for management to proactively address investor concerns. Addressing such concerns in advance of being asked about them not only inspires investor confidence but also enables companies to better control the message. It's a good exercise for board members to consider asking management in advance of earnings calls what officers believe are the most significant investor concerns, and how they intend to address them on the upcoming call.

- *Q&A protocol.* Sometimes the question and answer portions of earnings calls can become contentious, and it's precisely during those moments that officers are graded by investors for their decorum and professionalism. Unfortunately, less experienced small-cap officers often fall prey to: (1) interrupting one another; (2) answering questions specifically intended for other executives; (3) correcting one another; or (4) speaking over one another. Boards should consider providing advice to less experienced officers about the loss of credibility that results from any such breaches in protocol.

The **key point** here for directors is that small-cap companies often operate with such small margins of error that they simply can't afford to make poor impressions on investors during earnings calls. As is clear from the problems listed above, this is not "rocket science." Rather, for small-companies hosting earnings calls that inspire investor confidence is as much about preparation and thoughtfulness as it is about the actual financial results.

SOCIAL MEDIA

While the value of social media as a tool for public companies of all sizes is well recognized, public company boardrooms are becoming increasingly focused on the risks related to social media as opposed to the benefits. Larger public companies, assisted by specialized teams of consultants, have made considerable strides toward not only crafting comprehensive social media policies, but, more importantly, creating procedures and controls to enforce the policies. Small-cap companies, though, with their constrained budgets and more diminutive infrastructures, have struggled in some cases to establish policies or procedures that address the risks associated with social media. Therefore, many small-cap companies are at risk of either confusing investors, or, even worse, being exposed to liability.

Part of the problem for many small-cap boards is simply a lack of sensitivity to the risks. That is, specialized consultants, who do a great job of educating larger company boards about social media and sensitizing them to the risks, are unaffordable for many small-cap companies. Therefore, small-cap directors, many of whom have never used social media, are left to do their best with available resources and assistance from counsel.

There has been an enormous amount written about the risks to public companies posed by social media by academics, attorneys, consultants, and business commentators. Since this is not a treatise on social media, it suffices here to say that small-cap directors should, at a minimum, be mindful of the SEC's 2008 interpretive note on electronic communications.[12] In its note, the commission made clear that, among other things, all communications made on behalf of a company—even those made by employees on social media, blogs, and shareholder forums—are subject to relevant provisions of federal securities laws. In order for small-cap officers and directors to get a basic understanding of how Street confusion and various risks could arise, consider the following hypothetical situation.

XYZ is a public company that manufactures widgets. XYZ has an investor relations manager and several employees throughout the organization who are authorized to contribute to XYZ's website, XYZ's industry blog, and XYZ's Facebook and Twitter accounts. These employees also occasionally post on their own Facebook and Twitter accounts. XYZ is planning on releasing its quarterly earnings press release at 1 p.m. eastern time (during market hours) on its website; its earnings are far in excess of consensus estimates. At 12:50 p.m. a third-party financial blog that follows XYZ posts a note to the financial blog's Facebook page stating that its "channel checks weren't impressive—going to be a tough quarter for XYZ. But we love their new ABC 5000 widget which will be a HUGE winner for them." At 12:52 p.m., Sally, from XYZ sales and marketing, replies on the financial blog's Facebook page that she "likes" this posting, and puts a link to that Facebook page on XYZ's industry blog. At 12:54 p.m., Jim, also from XYZ sales and marketing, responds to a pejorative tweet about XYZ posted by a friend who works for XYZ's largest competitor, by posting a link on his personal Twitter page to a summary of a third-party analyst note reiterating that XYZ is a "strong buy." At 12:56 p.m., Larry, XYZ's investor relations manager, updates XYZ's official Facebook and Twitter pages to remind people that the earnings release is forthcoming, but erroneously instructs people to look for the release on the wire instead of on XYZ's website. The earnings release is posted on XYZ's website precisely at 1p.m. but isn't picked up by the wire services until 1:03 p.m. During the three-minute gap, the stock rises 10 percent. Later that afternoon, Margaret and some of her overworked, dissatisfied colleagues in XYZ's factory intentionally and untruthfully tweet in their personal Twitter accounts that the ABC 5000 is being shipped with a critical design flaw. The next morning, one of the research analysts covering XYZ elects to downgrade the stock because of the prior day's price increase. But since it's not good news, Larry decides not to say anything about that on XYZ's website or Facebook or Twitter accounts.

As fanciful as it might sound to officers and directors who are not social media savvy, fact patterns like this play out routinely, and the problems created in the process can be vexing. For example, although Sally might not have been intentionally seeking to mislead investors, what does it mean to an XYZ investor when an XYZ employee says they "like" a financial blog posting which predicts, among other things, doom for

XYZ's impending quarter; what if XYZ investors relied on that and sold their stock eight minutes before a 10 percent rally? Similarly, Jim might not have intended to mislead his Twitter followers by directing them to a summary of a positive analyst report, but are there ramifications to XYZ for its employee omitting regulatory disclaimers in connection with what can be construed as investment advice? Larry didn't intend to misguide investors by directing them away from XYZ's website for the earnings release, but having done so the three-minute news lapse could well have been costly to certain investors given the stock movement. Were the intentionally false and misleading tweets by Margaret and her colleagues made by or on behalf of XYZ? Is Larry's purposeful omission of the analyst downgrade actionable if XYZ's website and Facebook and Twitter accounts are, by design, places where the preponderance of XYZ's investors are encouraged to get their information about XYZ?

Whether attuned to social media or not, a practical approach for small-cap officers and directors to start evaluating the risks is to consider discussing a hypothetical like the one presented here and determine how and to what extent there are procedures in place to effectively manage these and other risks.

In conclusion, whether dealing with social media, press releases, or earnings calls, small-cap directors need to be vigilant and proactive about management's communication with the Street; avoiding common mistakes is a good starting point.

Notes

1. Though applicable to communications with all investors, this chapter is primarily geared to communicating with institutional investors. Where there are unique situations that arise in communicating with retail investors, they will be noted. Because communicating with investors during and after a financing and communicating with analysts were covered elsewhere in this book, those situations are not reiterated in this chapter.

2. Although there are regrettably circumstances in the small-cap realm where management intentionally overpromises in order to increase the share price and sell stock (euphemistically referred to as a "pump and dump" scheme), this tenet is intended to address the more common situation where the action is unintentional.

3. There is a litany of reasons why a company mightn't provide 100 percent transparency on a given issue to investors, including, but not limited to, regulatory/legal issues, competitive reasons, and operating within the confines of the other communications axioms.

4. Small-cap officers and directors should consider involving counsel in any situations in which investors (who are neither officers nor directors) are seeking to control or influence management, regardless of their stock ownership percentage. That is, there are often situations in which investors who own, for example, less than 10 percent of a company's issued and outstanding shares wield demonstrable influence over management, yet also freely trade the company's stock. Under applicable federal securities laws (e.g., Rule 405 of the Securities Act of 1933, and Rules 12 and 13 of the Exchange Act of 1934), it's plausible that such investors could be deemed "affiliates" after examining all the relevant facts and circumstances and therefore have diminished abilities to buy and sell the company's stock.

5. Hedge fund compensation is often described as "two and twenty." This means that hedge fund managers are collectively paid an annual fee of 2 percent of the assets under management and a performance fee of 20 percent of the yearly profit (if any, and typically adjusted to reflect any prior year's losses). Depending upon how funds account for and accrue the performance fee, there could well be times throughout the year when fund managers would benefit from the stock price being higher as opposed to lower for long positions or more liquid to facilitate monetizing positions.

6. In addition to alienating current and prospective shareholders, a steady flow of immaterial press releases also all but ends the company's chance of garnering impactful research coverage; that is, it will cause most experienced analysts to have trepidations about management's integrity. Additionally, companies that frequently issue immaterial press releases risk attracting the attention of regulators.

7. An example of an endorsement that could perhaps be viewed by the board and company counsel as material would be if a famous investor (e.g., George Soros, Carl Icahn, or Warren Buffett) spoke specifically and positively about the company, or if the company was featured on an iconic show like *60 Minutes*. Such endorsements are extremely rare. Rather, what most often gets repurposed in press releases by small-cap companies are positive comments from a blogger who believes that a company's stock is undervalued.

8. Part of handling subpar news with aplomb is making sure that management's commentary is appropriate to the circumstances. For example, investors rarely want to read the company's CEO state they are, "Very pleased with the company's results this quarter," when the company lost money. Why would any investor want to invest in a company in which the CEO is content with no profit? While somewhat of an esoteric observation, it's often a bone of contention for small-cap institutional investors, and it illustrates a common practice that companies and investors view very differently.

9. Under certain circumstances, a stock exchange or regulatory body might require a company to publicly respond to various reports, accusations, or unusual trading activity. The discussion that follows assumes that this is not the case and that the company's public reply, if any, is optional.

10. While accurately setting forth reasons why a stock might be overvalued is as important to the capital markets as setting forth compelling reasons to buy a particular stock, some stock blogs are little more than thinly veiled attempts to manipulate markets. The authors of the blogs (or related parties) have recently bought or sold the subject company's stock short, or purchased call or put options in advance of publishing the story with the goal of capturing a short-term profit caused by the predictable postpublication change in the stock price. Because fear sometimes has a more striking effect on small-cap stocks than optimism, purposely inflammatory short-biased blogs can often be considerably more impactful than long-biased pieces.

11. Replying can create an expectation that every time someone says something negative about the company in the marketplace, the company will publicly reply (and if the company doesn't reply, then perhaps investors will think that the accusations or innuendo are true because of the company's ensuing silence).

12. "Commission Guidance on the Use of Company Websites," Exchange Act Release No. 34-58288 (August 1, 2008).

CHAPTER 12

TOWARD A BETTER UNDERSTANDING OF STOCK BUY-BACKS AND REVERSE STOCK SPLITS

Buy-Backs and Reverse Splits

Key considerations for directors:

- Buy-backs and reverse stock splits are often better in theory than in practice—especially for many small-cap companies.
- Historic data are the best tool for directors to use in gauging the likely effectiveness of buy-backs and reverse stock splits.
- Buy-backs often don't succeed in stock price appreciation for many small-cap companies.
- Reverse stock splits to maintain senior exchange listings face uphill battles.

Common mistakes to avoid

- Relying on advisors instead of data to help analyze the likely effectiveness of buy-backs and reverse stock splits.
- Undertaking buy-backs in the absence of earnings per share and analyst coverage.
- Authorizing reverse stock splits in the absence of other seminal business news.
- Authorizing one-time cash dividends.

S mall-cap companies try a variety of different things, often under pressure from investors, in order to increase share price and either retain or change the exchanges where their stock is listed. While investors' motivations are always clear, the analysis of these corporate actions by small-cap officers and directors often is not.

Small-cap boards authorize scores of stock buy-backs and reverse stock splits (i.e., using the company's cash to repurchase its common stock on the open market, and with shareholder approval decreasing the amount of shares a company has outstanding) every year with the best of intentions and based on sound *theory*. That is, stock buy-backs are commonly transacted by Fortune 500 companies, and reverse stock splits are more an exercise in mathematics than a capital markets strategy. But, theories that apply elsewhere or otherwise intuitively make sense don't always work in the world of small-cap stocks.

DATA TRUMP THEORY

With the frequent absence of capital markets expertise on many small-cap boards, directors are understandably influenced by a variety of sources in making capital markets decisions—colleagues, investors, bankers, investor relations professionals, and attorneys, among others. One thing is quite certain. Board members of small-cap companies (especially small-cap companies with market capitalizations below $500 million) rarely consult historic data in making decisions about stock buy-backs and stock splits. If they did, buy-backs and reverse stock splits would be authorized a lot less frequently.

Rather than spending time and money soliciting opinions about buy-backs and reverse stock splits, many small-cap directors would do better by reviewing publicly available data. In other words, wouldn't any board find it helpful if the last 10 substantially similar companies that undertook stock buy-backs or reverse stock splits were trading at either the same stock price or lower (on an adjusted basis in the case of stock splits) 12 months after the buy-backs and reverse stock splits? Theory and diverse opinions are certainly valuable in assessing any board challenges, but when it comes to small-cap corporate finance and capital markets, data are where the rubber hits the proverbial road.

Upon review of relevant data, many small-cap boards would undoubtedly be surprised to find that buy-backs or reverse stock splits undertaken by similar companies have had mixed results at best and in many cases deplorable results for reasons that are unique to the small-cap ecosystem.

TIP

One of the most interesting insights into the effectiveness of small-cap stock buy-backs and reverse stock splits comes from the unlikeliest of sources—the negative covenants contained in most restricted stock financings. Embedded within the vast majority of restricted stock purchase agreements utilized in small-cap financings are, among other things, prohibition of two things—stock buy-backs, and reverse stock splits. While there is a variety of reasons why, implicit in those prohibitions is the fact that even though these corporate actions might at first lead to stock appreciation, the results can sour more often than not. Since investors with restricted stock can't easily sell the stock until it's registered (or otherwise unrestricted), they don't want to be bound to a sinking ship with no ability to escape. Food for thought for any small-cap directors considering buy-backs and reverse stock splits.

STOCK BUY-BACKS[1]

RATIONALE

The rationale for stock buy-backs in the small-cap realm is the same as it is elsewhere: to increase the share price by displaying confidence to the market that the company thinks its shares are undervalued, and by decreasing the number of shares outstanding (thus boosting earnings per share).[2]

WHY THEY OFTEN DON'T WORK[3]

- *Weakness.* Many small-cap companies come to the decision to undertake a stock buy-back because they are under tremendous pressure from investors because the stock is performing poorly. Therefore, small-cap stock buy-backs often take place from a position of weakness rather than strength. While boards are considering authorizing stock buy-backs under these circumstances, an equal amount of time should be spent analyzing why the company is in the weakened position in the first place. In other words, taking steps to remedy problems that might have contributed to a diminished stock price might ultimately create more shareholder value than the envisioned buy-back.

- *Questionable use of cash.* Most small-cap investors decide to invest in small-cap companies in order to capture the outsized multiples that can be afforded high-growth companies (as opposed to value investing). And, sure as day follows night, many high-growth companies need cash. Therefore, most small-cap investors would prefer to see growth companies retain their cash to propel further expansion rather than buy back stock. If a company is growing but either generates dramatic amounts of cash flow or already has an outsized cash balance, most investors would rather that the company simply return the cash to investors in the form of a dividend, rather than spend it buying back the company's stock. On the other hand, if a small-cap company isn't growing fast (and thus likely won't need the excess cash to fuel growth), then, like many slower-growth small-cap companies, it probably isn't sufficiently well followed for the buy-back to succeed.

- *No "E" in Earnings Per Share ("EPS").* An astonishing number of small-cap companies undertake stock buy-backs regardless of the fact that they have no earnings. If the company has no E then the number of S is neither here nor there, inasmuch as the company isn't being valued on a multiple of earnings per share.[4] The reality for many diminutive small-cap companies is that, in the conspicuous absence of earnings, they are valued more based on multiples of revenue, and valuations based on revenue are largely unaffected by share repurchases. Even in situations in which small-cap companies do have earnings, they might be largely held by retail investors and have no research coverage. In such situations, any attendant increase in earnings per share will have a muted effect.

- *Small dollar increments.* Many small-cap stock buy-backs are authorized in such small dollar increments relative to the number of shares outstanding that even if the company has earnings and is well followed, the impact on the company's stock price could well be marginalized.

Given these challenges, small-cap directors should approach stock buy-backs with some trepidation and make sure that the board has discussed these questions: (1) What's happened to the stocks of the last five to ten similarly situated companies that have authorized buy-backs? (2) Is this really the best use of the company's cash? (3) If the company doesn't have earnings, why does the board feel like a stock buy-back is going to create value for the shareholders? (4) If the company does have earnings but its stock is mostly held by retail investors and has no analyst coverage, is anyone going to even notice the stock buy-back? (5) Is the authorized amount of the buy-back large enough to actually make it worthwhile to undertake?

TIP

Another corporate action that's closely related to share buy-backs that small-cap directors often struggle to effectively analyze is declaring and paying cash dividends. The rationale for paying a cash dividend is relatively simple: the company doesn't have a present or envisioned use for the cash so it plans to return it to shareholders. The reason why small-cap directors understandably approach cash dividends with caution is that it's simply uncharted territory for most small-cap companies. When many small-cap companies have extra cash, they are usually going to need it so parting with it is anathema.

Small-cap companies that are going to pay a cash dividend need to be realistic about the expected results. Small-cap investors invest predominantly for growth, not for income. Therefore, it's unlikely that paying a cash dividend in and of itself is going to meaningfully augment trading volume or the stock price beyond the near term. In other words, growth stocks attract growth investors only when they are growing.

Additionally, if a company is going to see a sustainable uptick in trading volume and investor interest, this mostly likely will not happen with a large, one-time dividend for the same reason that companies that are launching a new product don't spend the entire advertising budget on a single advertisement. In other words, typically the most impactful results are achieved through a modest one-time cash dividend (if the company feels that "rewarding" long-time investors is necessary or will be fruitful) followed by a regularly paid cash dividend thereafter, or simply a regularly paid cash dividend.

But, again, if the company is otherwise not performing well, this is unlikely to meaningfully differentiate a small-cap stock from that of its peers in an ecosystem where investors seek growth, not income.

REVERSE STOCK SPLITS[5]

Reverse stock splits typically occur in three different small-cap settings: (1) to increase a company's share price in order to retain its listing on a senior stock exchange (i.e., maintain compliance with threshold minimum bid price listing requirements); (2) to increase a company's share price to make it more attractive to institutional investors and analysts; and (3) to increase a company's share price to move from a junior exchange listing to a senior exchange listing.

RETAINING A LISTING

It's quite common in the small-cap universe for a company's stock price to fall below the minimum bid price requirements of senior stock exchanges (e.g., NYSE and Nasdaq). Typically when this happens companies are given a period of time to regain compliance with the listing requirement; if the company doesn't comply, its stock can be delisted. While delisting is usually not a good thing for a small-cap company[6] small-cap boards rarely spend time evaluating the consequences of delisting. In other words, there can be circumstances in which delisting might actually be beneficial. For example, if a company needs to raise a substantial amount of capital, junior exchanges very often don't have "20 percent" rules thus facilitating much larger financings than might be possible on a senior exchange without shareholder approval. In the alternative, for most companies, and specifically for companies that don't anticipate material financings or for companies in which delisting can be financially penal,[7] small-cap boards often consider any and all options to retain senior exchange listings:

- *Rarely a positive outcome.* Unfortunately, reverse stock splits undertaken exclusively to retain stock listings aren't often successful in the longer term for several reasons: (1) short sellers often prey upon companies that undertake reverse stock splits in order to salvage stock listings because they are essentially handed stocks that are probably not performing well to begin with and are granted more "altitude" from which to fall; (2) the effects of short selling are often exacerbated by retail investors who don't understand reverse stock splits and so sell their shares postsplit because they believe erroneously that the value of their holdings has increased due to the higher stock price; and (3) a common, albeit unintended consequence of reverse stock splits is a loss of trading volume which amplifies the selling pressure.

- *Best chance for success.* Companies that successfully retain senior exchange listings with reverse stock splits over the longer term tend to: (1) announce the reverse stock split simultaneously with seminal, transformative corporate news (i.e., dramatic profitability, blockbuster Phase III clinical results, etc.); or (2) otherwise dramatically improve corporate performance postsplit.

Making Stock More Attractive

Although less common than reverse stock splits designed to retain senior exchange listings, small-cap companies sometimes effectuate a reverse stock split in order to increase the share price to a range that might make the stock more attractive to institutional investors and equity research analysts. Although "penny stock" rules have gone through various revisions since they were first enacted in 1990,[8] it suffices to say that there are still many institutional investors who won't buy stocks at under $5 a share or even stocks under $10. There are, correspondingly, equity research analysts who won't cover those stocks.

Reverse stock splits principally designed to increase the company's share price to make it more institutionally appealing have the same risks as splits designed to maintain senior exchange listings. They are most likely to succeed when they are undertaken by well-performing companies that have constrained share prices resulting principally from bloated share counts. Directors considering a reverse stock split have to weigh the benefits against the likelihood of attracting short sellers and decreasing the amount of daily trading volume.

Uplisting

Moving a stock listing from a junior exchange to a senior exchange can be a meaningful step in a public company's evolution, provided that the company is financially and operationally prepared for the transition. The

key point for directors considering an uplisting that's facilitated, in part, by a reverse stock split is that this strategy has the best chance of success in companies that have sustainable growth and are performing well.[9] Put differently, if the company is not growing, has little growth visibility, and is otherwise struggling operationally on a junior stock exchange, it's very unlikely that conditions will improve by moving the stock to a senior stock exchange (and the ability to undertake financings will also be more restrictive). Moreover, the same reverse stock split caveats discussed previously apply here.

CONCLUSION

Ultimately, small-cap directors need to rely more on data when it comes to stock buy-backs and reverse stock splits than advice. If other similarly situated companies have recently attempted the same things and the results have been poor, why is the company going to succeed where they failed? Alternatively, if other similarly situated companies have succeeded recently in this regard, boards should try to identify the reasons why they succeeded and objectively determine whether the company can similarly benefit.

Notes

1. For purposes of this discussion, this is also intended to include modified dutch auction tender offers. In a modified dutch auction tender offer the company's goal is the same as in an open market stock buy-back, but instead of buying back its stock in the open market the company provides a price range for how much the company will pay for a specific number of shares. Investors then tender their shares at a price within the range that they are willing to sell their shares.

2. Interestingly, small-cap companies that are inactively traded can actually boost their share price, at least temporarily, simply by virtue of repurchasing shares in the open market.

3. This discussion doesn't broach other hot button issues with buy-backs (e.g., is it ultimately management that benefits most from buy-backs, and associated conflict of interest issues). Also, this discussion doesn't differentiate between gross and net

buy-backs (i.e., sometime a share repurchase of 2 million shares doesn't have the net result of decreasing the outstanding share count by 2 million shares when the company simultaneously issues an equal or great number of employee stock options). Rather this discussion is purposefully intended to focus on the uniquely small-cap aspects of buy-back efficacy.

4. The main rationale behind stock buy-backs is to reduce the number of shares so that a company's earnings per share will rise. That is, if a company has earnings of $1 million and it has 10 million shares outstanding, its earnings per share are $0.10. If the company repurchases 2 million shares, then the earnings per share will be roughly $0.13. If the EPS multiple being applied to the company is 20, then the stock price should theoretically rise from $2.00 to $2.60.

5. A reverse stock split entails reducing the number of shares that a company has issued and that are outstanding. If the company's stock currently has a market capitalization of $100 million based on 100 million shares outstanding and a $1 stock price, it will have a $5 stock price and 20 million shares outstanding immediately following a one-for-five reverse stock split.

6. Delisting from a senior exchange typically results in materially less trading volume, lost research coverage, and share price erosion resulting from, among other things, institutional investors exiting positions that they can't maintain by mandate.

7. For example, small-cap financing documents often require companies to retain their senior exchange listings. If those requirements are breached, then notes could become immediately due and owing, or other penalties might begin accruing.

8. The Penny Stock Reform Act of 1990 sought to protect individual investors from purchasing stocks in nascent, risky companies by requiring, among other things, special disclosures from broker-dealers to investors setting forth the dangers of such investments.

9. It's even better if the company times the uplisting to coincide with seminal business news or a financing that provides the company with a healthier balance sheet.

PART 3

PROFESSIONAL
SERVICE
PROVIDERS

As discussed in Parts One and Two, small-cap companies fundamentally differ from larger public companies because they often require access to equity capital markets in order to augment either sustained or periodic negative cash flow. Consequently, every corporate action or omission that can impact access to capital has business-ending possibilities for many small-cap companies.

Effectively hiring and managing professional service providers is another good example, among others in Parts One and Two, of corporate action that rarely requires board oversight at larger public companies but that carries austere enterprise risk for many small-cap companies if executed poorly. More specifically, the advice provided by investor relations professionals, attorneys, and auditors[1] can not only be impactful on day-to-day operations, but their advice can also meaningfully affect the availability and cost of capital. For example: (1) poor Street communication practices can directly influence trading volume and stock price; (2) poor legal advice in connection with a financing can increase dilution, jeopardize senior exchange listings, and denigrate subsequent financing alternatives; (3) a combination of poor legal and audit work can delay or obviate regulatory approvals (e.g., registration statements); and (4) poor audit work can dramatically tarnish corporate credibility.

Unfortunately, such challenges with service providers are commonplace—every small-cap veteran has countless examples of small-cap companies that were driven to the brink by investor relations, law, and auditing firms that were either unaffordable or not sufficiently expert to provide the unique advice required.

There are two principal reasons why this happens often to small-cap companies: (1) the firms are often being retained and managed by officers who themselves don't have experience in investor relations, law, and public company accounting; and (2) as discussed in the Introduction, the quality of professional service providers in the small-cap realm is highly variable. And, to compound this dynamic, there are also many small-cap directors who lack appreciable capital markets, legal, and accounting acumen.

Therefore, the purpose of Part Three is to provide directors with a better understanding of how to assist management in expertly vetting, scoping, and managing these service providers.

CHAPTER 13

EFFECTIVELY HIRING AND MANAGING INVESTOR RELATIONS FIRMS

Getting the Most from Investor Relations

Key considerations for directors:

- Small-cap companies often start out on the wrong foot with IR firms.
- Companies and IR firms are equally to blame for some of the recurring problems that can plague these relationships.
- It takes time and effort to objectively identify where a company needs help communicating with the Street.
- Hiring IR firms should be part quantitative and part qualitative.

- Managing IR firms takes patience and vigilance.

Common Mistakes to avoid:

- Being too cynical or having unrealistic expectations.
- Not scrutinizing past performance or adequately checking references.
- Failing to thoroughly vet account managers as much as firm owners.
- Contributing insufficient energy and focus to the relationship.
- Being too deferential to advice.

Many small-cap companies approach investor relations (IR) with a sense of dread, as if it were a necessary evil or simply a cost of being a public company. Consequently, companies often cycle restlessly between different investor relations firms, and the relationships can sometimes become underwhelming self-fulfilling prophecies. But it shouldn't be this way, and directors can help management to make sure it isn't. Companies and investor relations firms are equally to blame for their problems most of the time.

COMPANY'S SHARE OF THE BLAME

While small-cap companies are often quick to find fault with the services provided by investor relations firms, officers and directors need to recognize common shortcomings in how many small-cap companies approach investor relations.

- *All or nothing.* Small-cap companies often start relationships with investor relations firms with either too much cynicism or too much fanciful expectations. In other words, the relationship is going to be a total waste of time, or the firm is going to completely transform the company's valuation and shareholder base—all or nothing. The reality, however, is that it's not all or nothing. For companies that are performing well, investor relations firms can augment a company's capital markets profile. For companies that are performing more moderately, investor relations firms can help maintain the status quo and help lay the foundation for more meaningful change if and when the company's results improve. For companies that are performing poorly, investor relations firms often can't provide palpable value, but they can provide strategic guidance on how the company can best take advantage of the opportunities it does have.

- *Matching purpose with need.* Small-cap companies often don't sufficiently understand what services investor relations firms can provide. Moreover, this lack of understanding is sometimes amplified by the company's failure to objectively appreciate its own particular capital markets challenges.

- *Hiring.* When the company doesn't completely understand the variety of services investor relations firms offer, it is almost impossible for the company to hire the right firm. The problem is exacerbated when the company isn't realistic about what it needs.

- *Effort.* Because the confluence of these factors often results in lackluster investor relations performance, companies inevitably put less and less effort into ensuing relationships.

IR FIRM'S SHARE OF THE BLAME

Investor relations firms often are their own worst enemies and have certainly earned some of the cynicism about the efficacy of small-cap investor relations.

- *Overpromise.* Investor relations firms certainly share a meaningful portion of the blame by stoking company expectations. The small-cap investor relations industry is a competitive one, and in an effort to attract and secure business, investor relations firms are often guilty of overpromising and underdelivering.

- *Due diligence.* Because many investor relations engagements can be comparatively short-lived, some IR firms conduct minimal due diligence prior to executing a service agreement. Since much of the preliminary due diligence is uncompensated time that could be spent on other fee-generating work, there is also a financial inducement to do less as opposed to more diligence. What suffers is the ability of the IR firm to substantively understand the company's capital markets challenges and make a correspondingly reasoned determination of whether the investor relations firm is well-suited to help.

- *Hard conversations.* Because of how competitive the small-cap investor relations industry is, some IR firms shy away from having direct, critical conversations with company management and instead opt for relationship-smoothing deference instead.

- *Conflicts.* Some investor relations firms can be guilty of recommending that companies undertake courses of actions (e.g., media training, nondeal roadshows, etc.) that are highly profitable for investor relations firms regardless of whether they are timely or necessary.

Understanding how and why each party is often to blame in perpetuating unmet expectations is an important first step in changing this dynamic. The next step is for companies to objectively identify exactly what they need help with in the investor relations context—something with which directors can be of great assistance.

DEFINING WHAT'S NEEDED

Just as a seasick passenger isn't always the best judge of a ship's cuisine, management isn't always ideally suited to objectively assess how well the company communicates with the Street. Therefore, it's a good exercise for directors to work together with management to review each component of such communication and get management's input. Then the board members can independently discuss whether they're in agreement with management's assessment.

More specifically, officers and directors should evaluate, among other things, the following different elements of Street communication:

- Content and distribution of press releases

- Earnings call scripts, format, and attendance

- Quarterly regulatory filings

- Definitive Proxy Statements, shareholder meetings, and interfacing with proxy firms

- Quality and timeliness of processing inbound investor inquiries

- Size and diversity of the shareholder base (when compared to that of peers)

- Strategies for increasing the size and diversity of the shareholder base

- Equity research coverage

- Share price and trading volume (when compared to peers)

TIP

As discussed throughout Parts One and Two, there are certainly circumstances that arise in small-cap companies where neither management nor directors have capital markets experience. Companies in these situations would be well served to hire a cost-effective independent third-party (one that doesn't stand to gain or lose from its assessment) to assist the company with better characterizing its strengths and weaknesses in communicating with the Street. To the extent that the company has institutional investors and equity research analysts, board members can also discuss the relative merits of perhaps seeking feedback from them regarding the company's strengths and weaknesses.

One of the realities of small-cap life is that sometimes it's not so much that officers and directors feel that a particular element of Street communication is a weakness, but rather it's that there isn't enough staff within the company to adequately handle the communication. Therefore, it's not uncommon for small-cap companies, especially more diminutive ones, to essentially outsource the lion's share of Street communications to investor relations firms (rather than have these firms assist with only one or two tasks). This level of reliance naturally elevates the risks associated with hiring the wrong firm.

Regardless of whether a company is outsourcing all aspects of Street communication to an investor relations firm or just a particular component, objectively identifying what the company needs help with is the most important prerequisite to hiring the right firm. Although this seems intuitive, it's worth reiterating that scores of small-cap companies fail to dedicate the time and effort to objectively assess the company's needs and consequently are in no position to hire an investor relations firm.

HIRING THE RIGHT FIRM

Once the company objectively identifies the elements of Street communication that it needs help with, the company is properly positioned to identify investor relations firm candidates and then more closely review their qualifications.

IDENTIFYING CANDIDATE FIRMS

As discussed in the introduction to Part Two, there are *good* stocks and *bad* stocks in the small-cap ecosystem sometimes independent of underlying operating merits. The **key point** for officers and directors to focus on is that the goal of small-cap investor relations is to find the right firm to assist a company in creating a good stock or maintaining a good stock. Therefore, the first step in identifying candidate firms is for the company to review other small-cap companies with similar revenue and profitability profiles with an eye to identifying those that also have *good* stocks; that is, those that trade more volume, have more analyst coverage, and have better valuations than peers. There are many reasons why a company can have a *good* stock at any moment in time, and it might have nothing to do with its investor relations firm (e.g., charismatic management, industry that's currently "in favor," etc.). But, as part of this analysis, companies will likely discern a trend; that is, a certain subset of investor relations firms tend to be more involved with *good* stocks than *bad* stocks in any given cross-section of company sizes or industries. It is from within this subset that candidate firms should be selected.

TIP

A common question that officers and directors quite rightfully ask in relation to choosing an investor relations firm is whether or not it's vital that an investor relations firm have domain expertise (e.g., software, medical technology, gold mining, etc.). The answer is that it depends principally on two things.

1. *Exchange.* If a company is not listed on a senior exchange, the domain experience of an investor relations firm is unlikely to make a difference. Rather, the goal of investor relations firms for companies on junior exchanges is largely to assist the company with the everyday "blocking and tackling" of becoming a bona fide public company, as opposed to a company that's run like a private company but happens to have a ticker symbol.

2. *Market capitalization.* For companies listed on senior exchanges that have less than $250 million market capitalization, it's a sliding scale. That is, highly technical or highly specialized businesses can benefit from investor relations domain expertise, and less technical or less unusual businesses will benefit less from domain expertise. The rationale for this is that there is likely to be a limited investor audience for highly technical or esoteric companies of this size, and an investor relations firm with a track record of successfully reaching those investors could well pay dividends. Once a company gets beyond $250 million in market capitalization, investor relations domain expertise starts to be of greater value because the company will begin appearing on the radar screens of more highly specialized institutional investors.

A second question that is also commonly asked is whether a company should consider using the same investor relations firm used by a competitor. The answer is that it depends on which company has a better stock. If the competitor has a better stock, then the company might be able to benefit from being introduced to the same investors and analysts, and that benefit might outweigh the risks of commingling company information. If the competitor does not have as good a stock as the company, then the risks would likely outweigh the benefits.

VETTING CANDIDATE FIRMS

When it comes down to a more granular assessment of investor relations firms, the process becomes reminiscent of the vetting described in Chapter 3 for investment banks. Candidate firms that most likely will perform well are those that have *recently, successfully assisted substantially similar companies with the same tasks for which the company requires help*. This is why it's imperative for companies to first be clear about exactly what they need help with. For example, if a company principally requires help with courting new institutional investors and a particular candidate firm specializes in writing and distributing press releases, then this firm is likely not a good candidate. Therefore, when interviewing candidate firms, it's critical to focus on precisely the services that were provided to substantially similar companies in order to best quantify a firm's capability to assist the company. Additionally, since one small-cap company might have a predominantly retail investor base and another similar small-cap company could well have a predominantly institutional investor base, it's critical for companies to distinguish between the two when interviewing candidate firms. If a company largely has a retail investor base and the candidate firm principally has experience with more institutionally held companies, then, successful track record notwithstanding, that investor relations firm could well be of limited value to the company.

COMMON MISTAKES IN HIRING IR FIRMS

Small-cap companies can improve their experiences with IR firms by avoiding some common hiring mistakes.

- *Referrals.* Often an investor relations firm will be referred to an officer or director by a trusted friend or colleague. Although there is, of course, nothing wrong with this, the problem is that the reference needs to be contextualized. If the referring party works for a company that is not substantially similar to the company, then the referral may not be helpful. In addition, if the referred IR firm wasn't principally providing the services which the company requires then the referral might ultimately be of limited value.

- *Reference checks.* As is discussed repeatedly in Part One, directors need to make sure that management has spoken with numerous existing and former clients to get a sense of the candidate firm's strengths and weaknesses. There is no excuse for failure in this regard, although as also discussed in Part One, it's astonishing how common it is for references not to be checked. Furthermore, it's also wise for companies to request and verify that candidate firms and personnel have not been sanctioned by regulators for past securities-related infractions.

- *Full service.* Many small-cap investor relations firms advertise themselves as providing a full suite of services for clients. Upon closer inspection many of the noncore services might be thinly supported. For example, if a company is considering an investor relations firm principally for investor outreach and press releases but is also considering consolidating its public relations efforts within the investor relations firm in order to manage one firm instead of two, care should be taken to assess whether the investor relations firm "offers" public relations services, or "specializes" in public relations services. Put differently, a small, roadside motel might well have the pool it advertises, but it mightn't suffice for an avid swimmer looking to swim laps for daily fitness.

- *No quick fixes.* It's an inescapable fact that there are myriad unscrupulous investor relations firms catering to small-cap companies. The easiest rule of thumb for officers and directors to use is that seemingly compelling marketing hyperbole notwithstanding, there are no quick paths to having a *good* stock—none. There are no miracle technologies, databases, systems, investors, or mailing lists. If a candidate firm promises this, then the company should simply move on to other candidates.

- *Account managers.* The owners and founders of prominent, well-regarded small-cap investor relations firms are savvy, charismatic, and highly experienced. The problem is that they are often not the people who are going to be doing the lion's share of the work on the company's account. Therefore, the **key point** here for directors is that they need to make sure that management has also spent considerable time getting comfortable with the account managers who are going to be the company's primary liaison with the candidate firm.

- *Long-term contracts.* Companies should be leery of entering into long-term investor relations agreements which are challenging or penal for the company to exit.

- *Milestones.* Written agreements with investor relations firms should attempt to quantify the goals of the relationship so that both parties have means to assess effectiveness. Because insufficient thought often goes into the retention of investor relations firms, officers and directors have limited means to assess whether the relationship is beneficial or not. This can lead to two bad results: prematurely ending an investor relations relationship that is actually creating value, or letting less compelling relationships last too long.

MANAGING IR FIRMS

In one sense, managing investor relations firms is no different from managing other professional service providers; that is, frequent, frank communication and close monitoring are required. But there is often an extra challenge in the small-cap ecosystem because those managing the relationship might not be sufficiently expert in capital markets matters to effectively gauge what they are seeing and hearing. Therefore, directors should make sure that management is taking the following steps:

- *Data.* When investor relations firms either suggest or discourage a certain course of action, management should request examples to support the firms' recommendations; that is, trust but verify. Put differently, the company is unlikely to be the only similarly situated company that has either tried or discontinued certain practices or strategies. Therefore, it's highly instructive (though not necessarily determinative) for management to understand what's happened in the past under similar circumstances.

- *Fluidity.* Just as the capital markets are fluid, successful management of investor relations firms needs to be similarly fluid. That is, management needs to continuously discuss and confirm with investor relations firms whether the current strategy, for example, with investor outreach is appropriate given movements in the company's stock or the overall markets. In other words, strategies that might make sense in one market environment don't make sense in others. Therefore, both management and investor relations firms have to display a willingness to prudently adjust thinking and strategy.

- *Personnel.* If the company has problems with people working on its account, the issue needs to be quickly and frankly addressed. Like any professional service relationship, there often has to be an acceptable personality match for the relationship to succeed. Therefore, management needs to be vigilant about IR firm staffing.

- *Rapport.* Management needs to have an open, constructive line of communication with the owners of the IR firm to evaluate the progress of the relationship and the performance of the account managers. This again underscores the necessity of having contractual mechanisms for evaluating the efficacy of the relationship.

- *Street feedback*. Regardless of which services the investor relations firm is providing, it's often helpful to seek investor feedback about positive or negative changes that have transpired since an investor relations firm was retained.

COMMON MISTAKES IN MANAGING IR FIRMS

Even a prudently hired investor relations firm can underperform company expectations if managed poorly.

- *Garbage in, garbage out*. Investor relations is equal parts art and science. Therefore, the less effort and attention management invests in the relationship, the less likely it is to succeed. Investor relations firms often complain about the absence of management effort and attention, and appropriately so. In order to resolve the problem, small-cap directors can assist by requesting management to make regular presentations to the board about the progress of various investor relations initiatives. Moreover, the independent members of the board can also occasionally ask investor relations firms to provide periodic updates to the board without management present. Street communication is critical for most small-cap companies, and the expense of investor relations can be material; all the more reason for directors to assist management in getting the most out of a properly hired firm.

- *Takes time*. Depending upon the kinds of services being provided by an investor relations firm, the results often are not evident immediately. Consequently, management needs to be patient for the desired results to unfold.

- *Operations versus IR*. One of the rules of golf is that the ball must be played as it lies; it's also a rule of investor relations. That is, investor relations firms are not responsible for the company's operations or financial performance. They do the best they can with the results they are provided. Ignoring that reality, small-cap companies routinely try to hold investor relations firms responsible for how investors respond to disappointing financial results.

- *Too deferential.* Companies need to respectfully challenge the advice they receive from investor relations firms in order to confirm that it's appropriate for and consistent with the strategy that's been agreed upon.

TIP

One of the main areas where management need to challenge investor relations firms is outreach efforts to meet with prospective investors, and small-cap directors should know the most relevant questions to ask in this regard to make sure that such outreach is time well spent:

1. *Why now?* Investor relations firms should be able to provide a succinct reason why this is a good time to be meeting with investors. In other words, is it because of what's going on in the broader stock market, or is it timed to coincide with something inside the company?

2. *How do these investors fit?* Depending upon the strategy agreed upon by the investor relations firm and the company, it's important to understand how particular investors fit within that outreach strategy.

3. *What other stocks do they own?* Investor relations firms should be able to provide a clear snapshot of the other stocks that are owned by a particular investor; for example, has this fund displayed a previous predisposition to own stocks like those of the company?

4. *Who is a prospective investor meeting going to be with?* The more that is known about the portfolio manager's likes and dislikes prior to the meeting, the better the chance for a constructive meeting to take place. If the investor relations firm doesn't

know the portfolio manager, it's the firm's job to find out everything it can about the manager so as facilitate a successful,
worthwhile meeting.

5. *Can this fund buy the company's stock?* This is easily one of
the least asked but most critical questions in small-cap investor relations. As alluded to in Chapter 9, an enormous amount
of time and money is wasted meeting with fund managers
who simply can't buy the stock by mandate (e.g., not senior
exchange-listed, stock price is too low, or market capitalization is too low) or because of mathematical exigencies (e.g.,
stock is too inactively traded). Therefore, directors should make
sure that management periodically asks the investor relations
firm for the average position sizes of funds that the investor relations firm would like to introduce, and then do some math.
If the fund needs to buy a minimum of $1 million of stock, can it
buy that much of the company's stock in 10 trading days or less
while comprising no more than 15 percent of the average daily
trading volume? Most funds won't buy stocks that take more
than 5 to 10 trading days to acquire, and if they comprise more
than 15 percent of the daily trading volume, they run the risk of
pushing the stock price up. The answer: only if the company's
stock trades a minimum of approximately $667,000 per day.

The **key point** here for officers and directors is that good investor relations firms can be invaluable to small-cap companies, but companies
need to be interested, informed purchasers of investor relations services
and remain vigilant about the IR firm's performance.

Note

1. Investment banking is another critical professional service provider relationship for small-cap companies (see Chapter Three).

CHAPTER 14

GUIDE TO PURCHASING LEGAL SERVICES

Hiring the Right Attorneys at the "Right" Price

Key considerations for directors:

- Small-cap companies can't afford to hire the wrong attorneys or pay too much for legal services.
- The legal services marketplace has become a buyer's market.
- Choosing the "right" attorneys for corporate finance transactions is critically important.
- Most SEC reporting work should be purchased on a flat-fee basis, if possible.
- Litigation is a minefield for small-cap companies, especially those without in-house legal expertise.

Common mistakes to avoid:

- Flat fees might be cheaper than hourly billing but they also might not be.
- Using company counsel for corporate finance work even when they're not the most qualified.
- Failing to shop SEC reporting work to firms outside major markets.
- Being penny-wise and pound-foolish when it comes to managing litigation risk.

B ecause so many small-cap companies operate without in-house counsel and many officers and directors lack legal backgrounds, there is a constant risk of either hiring the wrong attorneys or paying too much for legal services. The goal of this chapter is to provide some insights into three common circumstances involving legal services where small-cap directors should consider asking more thorough questions.

CURRENT LEGAL SERVICES ENVIRONMENT

The law firm business model is in the midst of a historic transformation. After decades of hypergrowth and profitability fueled by healthy, deep-pocketed corporate clients, the financial crisis knocked law firms of all sizes on their proverbial heels. A combination of fear and fiscal austerity has turned the business of providing legal services into a buyer's market.

For small-cap companies already saddled with comparatively crippling costs of "being public," the evolution of the marketplace for legal services is unreservedly positive. But even in the face of a buyer's market, many small-cap companies aren't benefitting as much as they should.

For example, one of the most dramatic changes to the law firm model is an inexorable shift away from hourly billing to flat fees. That is, the frequency of use of flat-fee structures has nearly doubled at large law firms in only the last three years.[1] At a high level, this is beneficial to purchasers of legal services, because hourly fee billing can be susceptible to conflicts of interest (i.e., lawyers can be tempted to take more time to complete tasks than less because they are getting paid by the hour). But, the **key point** for small-cap directors is that just because a company is now paying a flat fee for particular services doesn't necessarily mean that the company is getting a better deal. Especially when it comes to clients with less legal acumen, law firms still do their best to construct flat fees that aren't demonstrably different from historic hourly fees when all is said and done.[2] Therefore, directors need to ensure that management is exercising sufficient care to confirm that any flat fees agreed upon are, in fact, more advantageous to the company and its shareholders than hourly fees.

Additionally, the buyer's market for legal services is also making it possible for considerably more small-cap companies to benefit from utilizing large law firms. But just like oil changes and tune-ups cost a lot more for expensive cars than for economy models, ancillary fees and expenses at larger law firms can dwarf these costs at smaller law firms. Therefore, small-cap directors should make sure that management is factoring in more than just otherwise attractive flat fees into an assessment to upgrade law firms (i.e., for an "apples-to-apples" comparison, management must compare the total cost of legal services, not just the flat fees for various projects).

TIP

To be clear, there is nothing undesirable about using small, regional law firms; the quality of legal work can be just as good if not better than at a larger law firm. And it can often be a fraction of the cost. However, small-cap directors need to be mindful of the fact that law firms that aren't well known to institutional investors and regulators can give rise to concerns and delay. Directors need to take this into account in assessing management's law firm choices, especially within the context of corporate finance.

The positive developments in the legal services marketplace for small-cap companies notwithstanding, there are three circumstances in particular that are always deserving of added director scrutiny.

PRINCIPAL LEGAL SERVICES DANGER ZONES

Whether a small-cap company has an in-house counsel and directors, officers, or other employees who are lawyers or it's at the opposite
end of the continuum, many small-cap companies tend to have similar challenges when it comes to purchasing legal services—sometimes
it's with respect to which lawyers to hire, sometimes it concerns how
much to pay, and other times it involves how to efficiently manage the
lawyers.

Corporate Finance

As alluded to in Chapter 1, one of the most impactful problems that a
small-cap company can create for itself in the legal services realm is to
hire the wrong attorneys to represent the company in connection with a
financing. Unfortunately, hiring the wrong attorneys is a common occurrence, and the damage can be appreciable. There are steps directors can
take to assist management avoid the problem:

- *Company counsel.* While it's understandable that the company's
  outside counsel is often the most logical choice to represent the
  company in a financing, they are only the right choice if they
  have *extensive[3], recent[4] experience representing similarly situated
  companies[5] in similar financings[6]*. In other words, company counsel
  might be a good choice, but they also might be a terrible choice.
  To put things in perspective, the hedge funds that are going to be
  investing in most small-cap financings are represented by lawyers
  who essentially do nothing else but represent institutional investors
  in small-cap financings. In other words, they have done dozens,
  if not hundreds of financings. Therefore, the fact that outside
  attorneys may be trusted advisors and know the company well is
  helpful on the one hand, but useless on the other hand if they aren't
  similarly expert in small-cap financings. The **key point** here for
  directors is that management shouldn't select existing company

counsel to represent the company in a financing out of allegiance or laziness; company counsel is the right choice only if they are the most qualified.

TIP

Management often is susceptible to assuming that it can't possibly go wrong selecting a large, international corporate law firm to represent the company in a financing. This assumption is wrong. Many of the largest law firms in the world predominantly represent large private and public companies. With respect to corporate finance, the lawyers in those firms could well have experience navigating some of the most complex finance transactions ever undertaken. However, if they don't have significant experience representing small-cap companies in private placements and public offerings, then their other experience is largely not applicable. For example, just because mechanics work on Formula One cars for a living doesn't mean that they are the best people to replace the brakes on a commuter car.

- *Actual attorney*. Regardless of the size and type of law firm, the other **key point** for directors is to confirm with management that the actual attorney who is going to represent the company has *extensive, recent experience representing similarly situated companies, in similar financings*. In other words, it's not sufficient if the law firm has such experience. Rather, the actual attorney representing the company is the person who needs to have the highly relevant experience. As is the case with all professional service providers, the firm is only as good as the person within the firm who is doing the lion's share of the company's work.

- *References*. Quantity doesn't always ensure quality. Therefore, directors should make sure that prior to retaining any new attorneys, management speaks with some of the attorney's recent clients. As alluded to elsewhere in this book, it's hard to overemphasize how important reference checking can be, especially when it pertains to something as critical as financings for small-cap companies.

'34 ACT REPORTING FEES

Given the dearth of cash and cash equivalents on the balance sheets of myriad small-cap companies, there is little room for overpaying professional service providers. However, scores of small-cap companies still pay law firms more than necessary for basic '34 Act reporting—the core legal work for small-cap companies.[7]

- *Flat fee.* In light of the changes in the legal services marketplace, small-cap companies should strongly consider negotiating flat fees for basic '34 Act reporting in lieu of continuing to pay hourly fees.[8] In addition, when soliciting bids for this work, directors should encourage management to include ancillary items like reviewing related press releases and perhaps even attending a fixed number of board meetings in the flat-fee. The **key point** here for directors is that they should confirm that management is aware of the issue and that the company isn't needlessly overpaying for this work.

- *Billable work.* When it comes to documents that are still commonly billed to small-cap companies on an hourly basis (e.g., corporate governance policies, stock purchase agreements, registration statements, definitive merger agreements, etc.) it is often cheaper to let outside attorneys draft these documents from start to finish for the company's review unless the company has a highly competent in-house attorney. In other words, companies with insufficient legal staff often end up actually spending more money on legal fees by trying to draft these documents internally for counsel's review.

TIP

One of the hardest things for those without legal backgrounds is to efficiently purchase legal services that are billed by the hour. How does someone who is not an attorney know whether the amount of time being billed on a given matter is appropriate? The short answer is—he doesn't. But, simply letting attorneys know that they are being carefully watched can pay dividends. For example, first, ask the attorney how long she expects a project to take. Then tell her to let her company contact know when she has worked three-fourths of that time and provide a revised update on the time necessary to complete the project. The company should let the attorney know that she is not to proceed beyond the forecasted time without first alerting the company contact and informing him of the reason for the extension. The purpose of the dialogue is to let the attorney know that the company expects her to exercise care in her estimates and that the company is watching the clock carefully. While companies need to exercise care not to micromanage or be penny-wise and pound-foolish with attorneys, the opposite is arguably worse; that is, simply turning attorneys loose on work that's hourly billed without any guidance or parameters.

- *Location.* Given the introduction of e-mail and web conferencing, the location of company counsel has become less and less important. However, too many small-cap companies still pay a premium in order to have counsel located near the company. Directors should be aware that both flat and hourly fees (and expenses) are often demonstrably less at branch offices of large law firms that are located outside major markets.

LITIGATION

The costs and outcomes of litigation pose material enterprise risk for small-cap companies. Consequently, for small-cap companies without appreciable in-house legal acumen, directors should consider focusing with management on some common high-level litigation mistakes that are easiest to avoid:

- *Litigation consultant.* For small-cap companies with no in-house counsel and minimal litigation experience, officers and directors should strongly consider hiring a seasoned litigation attorney as a consultant to assist with, among other things, selecting attorneys, negotiating fees, reviewing strategy, and managing the litigation process, etc.[9] In the vast majority of circumstances, the cost of the consultant will be paid for several times over with the resulting savings. The **key point** here for directors is that litigation often poses sufficiently austere risks for small-cap companies without the companies also trying to preside over all aspects of litigation with no or limited experience.

- *Selecting litigators.* Similar to the discussion about selecting appropriate counsel to represent the company in connection with corporate finance matters, the company's existing counsel could be a good choice, but might not be. Directors should encourage management to consider selecting litigation counsel that has not only recently demonstrated success with substantially similar cases but also in the same venue. To be clear, high-quality litigators can often successfully ply their skill and experience even to areas of the law where they have little prior experience. Small-cap companies often can't afford to take that risk and would be better served with counsel that has experience that's on point.

- *Alternative fee structures.* When the company is the plaintiff in a litigation, it should consider negotiating either a contingent fee or a blended contingent fee agreement with counsel instead of paying straight hourly fees.[10] Previously only the province of small specialty plaintiff's law firm, much larger law firms now regularly take cases using alternative fee structures.

When it comes to litigation for many small-cap companies, directors need to be aware of the fees and the outcome because both can be equally damaging. To that end, often the most important thing officers and directors can do when confronted with litigation is to be brutally frank about what they *don't* know.

TIP

A common source of confusion for many small-cap companies involves the decision about whether to hire an in-house attorney. The fundamental misunderstanding typically revolves around the business case; that is, the driving notion behind hiring a general counsel should be that, inclusive of the general counsel's salary, the company's entire legal costs will actually diminish. Therefore, to justify in-house counsel, the attorney should have the required expertise to do the company's most expensive legal work in-house. If the company is principally looking for less expensive legal work to be done in-house (e.g., contract work), then it's possible that it would be more cost efficient to hire a contracts administrator instead of a general counsel.

FIVE ADDITIONAL WAYS TO SPEND LESS MONEY ON CORPORATE ATTORNEYS

Even experienced in-house counsel can benefit from time-tested ways to decrease legal expenditures.

1. Don't use one law firm for all the company's work (i.e., when law firms know that the company isn't afraid to reassign work to other firms they will often work more efficiently to retain existing business).

2.   Become conscientious students of what other similar companies are paying for legal services, and insist that law firms continuously earn the company's business.

3.   When paying by the hour, make sure staffing excludes junior attorneys who are notoriously inefficient.

4.   Assume every lawyer addressed on an e-mail is billing the company for reading and acting upon the e-mail.

5.   Especially during litigation, negotiate in advance how much the company is willing to pay for courier service, litigation support, photocopies, office supplies, travel, and computer legal research.

Ultimately, the majority of small-cap companies cannot afford to either hire the wrong attorneys or pay too much for legal services. By more thoroughly exploring the company's choice with management, directors can minimize the enterprise risks.

Notes

1. Smith, J., "Companies Reset Legal Costs," *The Wall Street Journal*, April 9, 2012, p. B6 (citing a Citi Private Bank Survey).

2. For example, a law firm might quote a flat fee for all "'34 Act reporting" (e.g., 10Q, 10K, 8-K filings, and so on) to match a competitive quote from another law firm for the same work, but it may exclude legal work for preparing and filing a definitive proxy statement. Accordingly, the flat fee appears to be the same as what other companies are paying for annual regulatory filings, but it's not when you factor in the hourly billing on the proxy statement.

3. "Extensive" in this case means six or more financings.

4. "Recent" in this case means in the last twelve months. This is important, because small-cap regulatory rules and financing structures can change over the course of 12 months.

5. "Similarly situated companies" in this case means companies with similar capital markets profiles. This is important, because companies with smaller market capitalizations often face, for example, the complex "20 percent rule" problems that a lawyer used to representing large companies wouldn't necessarily be expert in navigating.

6. "Similar financings" in this case means the same type of structure. For example, if lawyers principally have experience representing small-cap companies in registered direct financings, they might not even know where to start in representing a small-cap company in an equity line or convertible note financing.

7. Examples of reports that must be filed either annually or quarterly pursuant to the Exchange Act of 1934 include, 10Q's, 10K's, 8K's, and DEF14A (proxy).

8. Although highly dependent upon the size of the company and its in-house legal capabilities, many small-cap companies now pay between $40,000 to $60,000 for these services on a flat-fee basis.

9. It's important to note that even for small-cap companies with an in-house counsel, if the in-house attorney doesn't have litigation experience then that attorney could well be of limited assistance to the company in a litigation context.

10. A typical contingent fee agreement provides that the attorneys absorb all the legal fees (costs are negotiable), and in exchange for this they receive 33 percent of the judgment prior to trial, 40 percent of the judgment if the case goes to trial, and 45 percent of the judgment if the case goes to appeal. A blended contingent fee agreement typically provides that the attorneys charge a substantially diminished hourly rate and then receive 20 percent of the judgment.

CHAPTER 15

AUDIT FIRMS: WHY IT PAYS TO THINK LIKE AN INSTITUTIONAL INVESTOR

The *Good* Stock "X" Factor

Key considerations for directors:

- Institutional investors, unlike most retail investors, place great emphasis on the integrity of financial statements.
- From an institutional investor perspective, an audit firm's reputation is critical.
- Not every audit firm is affordable for small-cap companies, nor is every audit firm interested in small-cap business.
- When evaluating candidate audit firms, small-cap companies should utilize the same assessment tools used by institutional investors.

- Ultimately, cost of capital and access to capital can be greatly affected by a small-cap company's audit firm.

Common mistakes to avoid:

- Underestimating how important audit integrity is to institutional investors.
- Failing to adequately weight an audit firm's Street reputation when considering an audit firm change.
- Jeopardizing a small-cap company's ability to have a "good" stock by remaining with an audit firm out of loyalty and comfort.

While retail investors typically don't spend a lot of time factoring a small-cap company's audit firm into their investment decisions, institutional investors do—and then some. Institutional investors invest predominantly in financial performance, and the reporting of financial performance is thorough, reliable, and accurate, or it isn't. Therefore, and not surprisingly, most institutional investors have fairly refined opinions about which audit firms are satisfactory, and which aren't.

And since they are ultimately the ones who write the checks—they don't call it the "buy-side" for nothing—small-cap companies which are otherwise well-suited to begin evolving their shareholder base from retail investors to institutional investors have little choice but to pay attention to investor preferences.

However, this creates an interesting conundrum for many aspiring small-cap companies. Large public companies typically choose from one of only four audit firms that are all affordable, acceptable to institutional investors, and highly solicitous of their business. Conversely, small-cap companies choose from dozens of audit firms, but depending upon the size and health of the small-cap company, most of the audit firms that institutional investors likely favor are unaffordable and might not want to audit riskier, smaller companies.

Therefore, the audit firm selection process in many small-cap company audit committees ends up being a Venn diagram with three principal inputs: affordability, the audit firm's willingness to audit, and the audit firm's reputation (see Figure 15.1).[1]

Two of the three inputs are easily gauged—an audit firm's affordability and its willingness to audit the company. The third—reputation—is where many small-cap audit committees understandably struggle to find the appropriate barometer and also to provide the proper weighting. While an audit firm's reputation means different things to different constituents, the austere reality is that only one group's opinion ultimately matters—institutional investors. The boards of aspiring small-cap companies can't afford to underestimate an ominous capital markets truism: the choice of

Figure 15.1 **Audit Venn diagram**

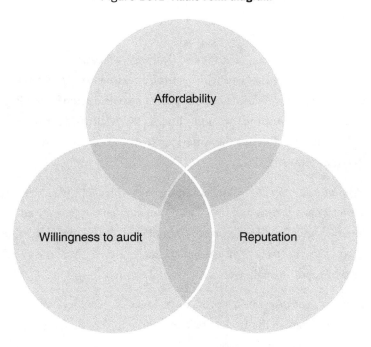

audit firms can prove to be an impediment to widespread consideration by institutional investors.

DEVELOPING A CANDIDATE POOL

Although it would be nice if institutional investors collectively published a list of all the audit firms that were on their "approved" list, they don't. There is no such list. But what small-cap audit committees can do, and should consider doing, is to apply the same criteria for choosing an audit firm that institutional investors do in order to develop a list of candidate firms. The best way for small-cap companies to choose from an institutional investor–approved pool of audit firm candidates is to think like an institutional investor.

There are four principal criteria that institutional investors weigh in evaluating audit firms:

- *PCAOB/peer audits.* One of the critical ways that audit firms develop good reputations with institutional investors is by having exceptional results from audits of their firm conducted by the Public Company Accounting Oversight Board (PCAOB), and through peer review entities like the American Institute of Certified Public Accountants (AICPA).[2]

- *Regulators and media.* When audit firms do their jobs well, they are typically not mentioned in the media or singled out by state and federal regulators. Therefore, the extent of the firm's public profile is typically inversely proportional to the regard in which the firm is held by institutional investors.

- *Industry expertise.* Like all professional service providers, audit firms often distinguish themselves by demonstrating particular expertise in auditing certain industries.[3]

- *Consensus.* Institutional investors constantly compare notes with one another and pull together what they've witnessed, read, and heard.

The **key point** here for small-cap audit committee members is that by striving to select a pool of audit firm candidates utilizing the same criteria as those applied by institutional investors, the company can be confident that the chosen firm will probably be acceptable to institutional investors.

THE *GOOD* STOCK "X" FACTOR

The purpose of this chapter is to underscore what is often overlooked. Because there are so many small-cap audit firms of such disparate quality, the choice of one audit firm over another can become the "X" factor, which contributes to one small-cap company having a *good* stock and another small-cap company having a *bad* stock.

Think of it from the perspective of an institutional investor. Gauging the strengths, weaknesses, opportunities, and threats to any small-cap company is perilous enough as it is. To then layer on concerns about the integrity of audited financial statements not only creates a fundamental issue of valuation, but an equally important matter of perception. In other words, even if a particular company's financial statements are perfectly accurate, a negative consensus about the company's audit firm among institutional investors is likely to create a negative feeling about the company's stock. Consequently, wherever there are concerns about the quality and reputation of audit firms, institutional investors will either invest less or not at all.

The **key point** here for directors is that the two things that matter most to myriad small-cap companies—cost of capital, and access to capital—can be significantly affected by the company selecting an audit firm that has an unsatisfactory reputation among institutional investors. Therefore, audit committees of small-cap companies that have institutional investors or seek to evolve their shareholder base from retail investors to institutional investors need to constantly reexamine whether the company's audit firm is the most institutional investor–friendly firm that the company can attract and afford. The alternative—sticking with an audit firm strictly out of loyalty or comfort—will rarely benefit shareholders.

Notes

1. These three principal inputs are not intended to be all-inclusive. Beyond affordability, the willingness to audit, and reputation, there are myriad important factors that ultimately determine the choice of one audit firm over another. Such factors include, but are not limited to, client references for audit partners, personality/rapport, geography, communication skills, staffing/turnover, and responsiveness.

2. The results of these audits are publicly available on PCAOB's and AICPA's websites.

3. Although high quality audit firms can apply their expertise to myriad industries, it's never advisable for a small-cap company to choose an audit firm that has little or no experience auditing a company in its industry, especially if that industry is known for highly nuanced accounting issues.

CONCLUSION

Bigger is better in the United States, and it probably will always be that way. But lest the "small-cap" nomenclature fool anyone, small-cap companies are "big" suppliers of innovation and "big" suppliers of U.S. jobs. In fact, they are "bigger" suppliers of U.S. jobs than most of the corporations for which the United States is best known around the world.

It's against this backdrop that this book has attempted to create a new awareness:

- An awareness that governing small-cap companies is not the same as governing larger public companies—not even close.

- An awareness that the "one-size-fits-all" approach to corporate governance not only doesn't work but is, in part, responsible for why our "big" suppliers of U.S. jobs chronically underperform.

- An awareness that the incessant need for growth capital creates governance challenges that are unique to small-cap companies.

- An awareness that dire enterprise risks are lurking around every corner for small-cap companies.

- An awareness that without this book, and considerably more content like it, small-cap directors will continue to struggle to help their companies live to fight another day.

If one of the chief lessons learned from the financial crisis was that directors will ultimately fail if they are continually asked to manage risks they don't sufficiently understand, then the corporate governance community hasn't learned very much. That is: (1) the vast majority of directors in the Unites States govern small public companies; (2) the vast majority of those companies are not cash flow positive and regularly need to access the equity capital markets to survive; (3) the vast majority of small-cap boards either can't afford to or don't have capital markets and corporate finance experts on their boards; and (4) the vast majority of small-cap directors are forced to simply "do their best" because there are no objective resources available to help them.

As discussed in the Introduction, being a small-cap director is an exercise in entrepreneurial governance—being nimble, doing more with less, and shepherding an asset against long odds for risk-embracing shareholders. Entrepreneurial governance often requires directors to call an audible at the line of scrimmage because the play called needs to be changed—quickly—in order to adjust to a new set of circumstances.

As it pertains to small-cap companies, the corporate governance community at large should consider calling an audible, meaning that the existing body of scholarship, best practices, and continuing education just isn't that helpful in addressing the continuum of challenges small-cap directors face. And every day that the audible isn't called, there is less innovation, and fewer American jobs.

INDEX

Note: Boldface numbers indicate tables and illustrations.

ABOUT THE AUTHOR

Adam J. Epstein is lead director of OCZ Technology Group, Inc. (Nasdaq: OCZ), and acts as a special advisor to numerous small-cap boards and investment funds through his firm, Third Creek Advisors, LLC (TCA).

Prior to founding TCA, Mr. Epstein cofounded and was a principal of Enable Capital Management, LLC (ECM). During his tenure there, ECM's special situation hedge funds invested in more than 500 small-cap financings in the United States, the European Union, and Australasia.

Before ECM, Mr. Epstein held senior operating roles with Enable Capital, LLC, a merchant bank; Surge Components, Inc., a vendor of discrete capacitors and semiconductors; MailEncrypt.com, Inc., a provider of encrypted e-mail services; Tickets.com, Inc., an entertainment ticketing company; and Achilles' Wheels, Inc., an operator of skate and snowboard retail locations.

He started his career as an attorney at Brobeck, Phleger & Harrison, after having been a law clerk at Willkie Farr & Gallagher.

Mr. Epstein has been featured in the *The Wall Street Journal* and on *CNN Presents*. He regularly writes small-cap corporate governance features for *Directorship*, is a member of the National Association of Corporate Directors, and is frequently a featured speaker at national corporate governance events.

Mr. Epstein earned a Juris Doctor from Boston University and a Bachelor of Arts, *cum laude*, from Vassar College. Preceding his undergraduate work, Mr. Epstein graduated from the American School in London.

CPSIA information can be obtained
at www.ICGtesting.com
Printed in the USA
BVHW040438171020
591234BV00005B/42